100+ INSPIRATIONAL *Short Stories* ABOUT SUCCESS *and* HAPPINESS

Insightful Words of Wisdom
to Motivate, Educate and Create
A More Empowered You

Compiled by:
VERUSHA ROBBINS | VIREND SINGH

Published by
Ink 'n Ivory
P O Box 6321, Rouse Hill, NSW. 2155. Australia

www.inkNivory.com
Blog: www.CoolSelfHelpTips.com

First Printing: 2025

ISBN: 978-1-922113-40-5 (Paperback)
ISBN: 978-1-922113-41-2 (ePub)
ISBN: 978-1-922113-42-9 (Hardback)

Disclaimer

This publication is shared with the understanding that the publisher and author are not engaged in rendering financial, psychological, or any other professional service and are offered for information purposes only. If financial or any other professional advice or assistance is required, the services of a competent professional person should be sought. The reader is solely responsible for his/ her own actions arising from the use of this document.

A Free Gift

A dad-and-daughter initiative to empower individuals to unlock their full potential and achieve their most extraordinary lives with the "hidden" laws of success and happiness.

CLASSIC EDITION
THE INEXPLICABLE LAWS OF SUCCESS
DISCOVER THE HIDDEN TRUTHS THAT SEPARATE THE 'BEST' FROM THE 'REST'
VERUSHA ROBBINS | VIREND SINGH

Download from leading online bookstores:
www.Chosen4U.com/tss

A Quick Tip to Maximize Your Learning

Unlock the Full Potential of "100+ Inspirational Short Stories About Success and Happiness."

As you embark on this journey to enrich your life through these life-changing stories, I want to share a life hack I found years ago.

While reading this book, I highly recommend pairing it with the audiobook version. By listening to the audiobook alongside this book, you'll be able to:

- Absorb the material more efficiently
- Retain more information
- Apply the principles to your life more effectively
- Experience a more immersive and engaging learning experience

To get started, secure your copy of the audiobook version of "100+ Inspirational Short Stories About Success and Happiness" from the options provided at the following link:

https://Chosen4U.com/SSAudio/

Contents

Introduction

Life is a wild ride full of unexpected twists and hurdles – some small, others fairly huge. When we feel overwhelmed, it's only natural to reach out and seek sources of inspiration and hope. That's where stories come in. There's something deeply magical about them – they pull us in, teach us something without lecturing, and stick with us long after we've closed the book or walked away.

If you are looking for the best inspirational and motivational short stories to guide you through life's obstacles, look no further. Inside, you'll discover true tales of ordinary people accomplishing incredible things. Parables that deliver ageless wisdom with a modern flare. Engaging fables that push you to think, reflect, and maybe even grow a little. Whether true or spun from pure imagination, each story is a spark ready to ignite your inner fire.

These stories don't just entertain; they're reservoirs of hard-earned wisdom, little reminders that you're not alone in this grand, sometimes chaotic life adventure. Think of these stories as traveling companions, here to inspire, educate, and empower you. Your journey starts now!

A Note from the Publisher:

We've poured our hearts into crafting this collection, ensuring each story – true, fictional, or a blend of both – shines brightly and speaks for itself. To further enrich your experience, you'll find a thought-provoking section titled "Ponder this:" at the end of each tale. Consider these like a gentle nudge to think a little deeper if that particular story strikes a chord. Connect with them if they are relatable, or skip past them and let the stories awaken your own insights. The choice is yours!

The Missing Contact Lens

Brenda, an adventurous young woman, embarked on her first rock climb with a group of friends. Despite her apprehension, she geared up, grasped the rope, and began ascending the imposing granite cliff. Halfway up, she reached a ledge – a welcome respite. As she clung to the rock face, the safety rope snapped against her eye, dislodging a contact lens.

Panic surged. Stuck hundreds of feet from both the ground and the summit, Brenda's vision blurred without her lens. She searched the ledge, without success. Desperation mounting, with a deep breath, she offered a prayer, seeking calm and guidance in finding the lost lens.

Reaching the top, a friend examined her eye and her clothing for the lens, but it was not to be found. Although she was calm now that she was at the top, she was despondent because she could not clearly see across the range of mountains. She recalled the biblical verse: "The eyes of the Lord run to and fro throughout the whole earth."

"Lord," she pleaded, "you see everything – every stone and leaf. You know where my lens is. Please help me find it."

As they descended the trail, they encountered a new group of climbers setting off. To their astonishment, one of them called out, "Hey! Did anyone lose a contact lens?"

This unexpected query was baffling enough, but the reason behind it was truly remarkable. An ant, diligently traversing a twig clinging to the rock face, was carrying Brenda's lost lens!

The story doesn't end there. Brenda's father, a cartoonist, was captivated by the tale of prayer, perseverance, and an industrious ant. He immortalized the scene in a cartoon: an ant struggling with the cumbersome contact lens, with the caption, “Lord, I don’t know why you want me to carry this thing. I can’t eat it, and it’s awfully heavy. But if this is what you want me to do, I’ll carry it for you.”

The recovery of Brenda’s lost lens goes beyond being just a lucky coincidence. It’s a testament to the power of faith and the potential for unexpected interventions from the universe.

Adapted from various versions on the internet.

Ponder this:

Life can throw big challenges our way, making us feel a bit lost. But if we hold onto faith and keep pushing forward, even the toughest problems can have surprising solutions. Whether it’s trusting in a higher power or just staying positive, it opens doors to amazing possibilities, sometimes through small actions we might not even notice.

This story teaches us that even tiny creatures can be part of a larger plan. It’s a reminder to trust that when things get tough, there might be unseen forces at work, helping us find answers in ways we might not expect.

The Unsolvable Math Problem

One day in 1939, George Bernard Dantzig, a doctoral candidate at the University of California, Berkeley, arrived late for a graduate-level statistics class and found two problems written on the board. He quickly copied the two math problems on the board, assuming that they were the homework assignment. It took him several days to work through the two problems, but he finally completed them. The next day he dropped the homework on the professor's desk.

On a Sunday morning a few days later, George was awakened early by a call from his excited professor. Since George had been late for that class, he hadn't heard the professor announce that the two problems on the board were mathematical mind-teasers that even Einstein hadn't been able to solve. But George Dantzig, believing that he was working on ordinary homework problems, had solved not one, but two problems that had stumped mathematicians for hundreds of years!

(Kersey, 1998)

Ponder this:

This story is not limited to the field of mathematics. It reminds us that most restrictions come from the inside. We set ourselves up for amazing feats when we tackle tasks with a "beginner's mind," devoid of preconceived assumptions of difficulty. Dantzig's tale not only encourages us to stay curious, think openly about problems, and work hard for solutions despite obstacles, but it also shows us that both natural talent and perseverance are key.

Lady, are you rich?

They huddled inside the storm door – two children in ragged outgrown coats.

"Any old papers, lady?"

I was busy. I wanted to say no – until I looked down at their feet. Thin little sandals, sopped with sleet. "Come in and I'll make you a cup of hot cocoa." There was no conversation. Their soggy sandals left marks upon the hearthstone.

Cocoa and toast with jam to fortify against the chill outside. I went back to the kitchen and started again on my household budget…

The silence in the front room struck through to me. I looked in.

The girl held the empty cup in her hands, looking at it. The boy asked in a flat voice, "Lady… are you rich?"

"Am I rich? Mercy, no!" I looked at my shabby slipcovers.

The girl put her cup back in its saucer – carefully. "Your cups match your saucers." Her voice was old with a hunger that was not of the stomach.

They left then, holding their bundles of papers against the wind. They hadn't said thank you. They didn't need to. They had done more than that. Plain blue pottery cups and saucers. But they matched. I tested the potatoes and stirred the gravy. Potatoes and brown gravy, a roof over our heads, my man with a good steady job – these things matched, too.

I moved the chairs back from the fire and tidied the living room. The muddy prints of small sandals were still wet upon my hearth.

I let them be. I want them there in case I ever forget again how very rich I am.

(Doolan, 1970)

Ponder this:

This story shows us a beautiful way to look at what real wealth means. Even though the kids didn't have fancy clothes or a lot of food, they saw something special in the woman's home – a feeling of everything fitting together just right. The cups matching might seem small, but they stand for a life where everything comes together nicely, and basic needs are taken care of.

The story teaches us that true wealth isn't just about having lots of stuff. The woman, even though she wasn't super rich, knew she had a lot to be thankful for: a loving partner, a cozy home, and a steady job. These everyday things made her feel safe and happy, and they also let her be kind to others.

The wet footprints left behind by the kids remind us of those who might not have as much. They made the woman appreciate the "matching" parts of her life even more – the things that make her life feel complete and steady. This story encourages us all to be grateful not just for material abundance, but for the simple blessings that make life good.

Snapshot at Lourdes

Carol Anderson was a young widow whose husband had died of cancer at thirty-five. Bob Edwards was a young widower whose wife had been killed in a car accident at twenty-nine. Both marriages had been extremely happy, and both Carol and Bob were sure they would never love or marry again. After many lonely years of pain and suffering, they met at a church dinner and started courting. When they got engaged and then married, they told everyone that it was miraculous that they had found each other. Their relationship was strong and loving. The only trouble spot in the marriage was that they had diametrically different opinions on what to do about the past.

Carol longed to bury it; Bob needed to explore it. Carol never wanted to talk about either of their previous marriages. Bob, on the other hand, was eager to know the minutest details of Carol's life before they had met, and was hurt that Carol showed such a complete lack of interest in his.

'Why raise ghosts?' Carol would ask when Bob would persist with his gentle probing and soft inquiries.

'Memory should be preserved, not obliterated,' he would reply. This went on for years, with Carol's perspective ultimately prevailing. As a result, they never shared stories, pictures, or mementos from their first marriages.

Ten years later, Carol felt their marriage was secure enough to withstand any assaults from the past. 'Okay,' she told Bob one day, 'I'm ready to talk.' She began telling Bob about her first marriage and pulled out several snapshots albums she had hidden from him all these years. 'These are from our honeymoon,' she said, starting to leaf through the pages of one album. 'We went to France. Oh, here we are at Lourdes.

'You went to Lourdes?' Bob said with mild interest. 'So did we.'

'Well, I guess half the world goes to Lourdes,' Carol laughed. 'No big deal. Everyone was looking for blessings and miracles in their lives.'

'Wait a second, Carol, turn back a page,' said Bob suddenly. 'Let me see the snapshot again of you and Ralph at Lourdes.'

Carol obligingly turned back a page.

'Carol," her husband asked tensely, 'who is that couple in the background?'

'I have no idea,' she said. 'Just as the photographer snapped the picture, a couple walked by and got caught by the shutter. I can see why you asked, though, thinking they were with us. In the picture it does look as though they're standing behind us, almost as if they're posing, but it's just an illusion.'

'You're wrong, Carol,' Bob said slowly. 'It wasn't a mistake, it was destiny. You see that couple in the background was me and my first wife.'

(Halberstam and Leventhal, 1997)

Ponder this:

The chance encounter captured in the photograph compels us to contemplate the nature of fate and coincidence. This seemingly random event raises questions about the interconnectedness of our lives and the possibility that some unseen forces may shape our journeys. Does this snapshot suggest a predetermined encounter between Carol and Bob, or is it simply a remarkable twist of fate? The story invites us to consider the role of chance and destiny in shaping our lives.

Growing Good Corn

There was a Nebraska farmer who grew award-winning corn. Each year he entered his corn in the state fair where it won a blue ribbon. One year a newspaper reporter interviewed him and learned that the farmer shared his seed corn with his neighbors.

'How can you afford to share your best seed corn with your neighbors when they are entering corn in competition with yours each year?' the reporter asked.

'Why sir,' said the farmer, 'didn't you know? The wind picks up pollen from the ripening corn and swirls it from field to field. If my neighbors grow inferior corn, cross-pollination will steadily degrade the quality of my corn. If I am to grow good corn, I must help my neighbors grow good corn.'

He was very much aware of the connectedness of life. His corn could not improve unless his neighbor's corn also improved.

The same is true in other aspects of life. Those who choose to be at peace must help their neighbors to be at peace. Those who choose to live well must help others to live well, for the value of a life is measured by the lives it touches. And those who choose to be happy must help others to find happiness for the welfare of each is bound up with the welfare of all.

The lesson for each of us is this: if we are to prosper, we must help others prosper.

Adapted from various versions on the internet.

Ponder this:

The farmer's tale shows us how connected everything is. Our own success doesn't happen in a bubble; it's about working together and lifting each other up. Just like how the farmer's crops did well when everyone's fields were thriving, we all do better when we support each other's growth and achievements.

You'll notice that the most successful folks are often the ones who've helped others the most. They understand that their rewards in life are in direct proportion to the services they render to others. True success isn't just about being the toughest or most competitive; it's about being cooperative and enjoying the journey together!

Thinking "Out of the Box"

This classic story, set in a quaint Italian town, showcases the triumph of wit over deceit. A merchant finds himself burdened by a heavy debt owed to a repulsive moneylender. The moneylender, driven by an unwelcome attraction to the merchant's beautiful daughter, proposes a repugnant solution: the debt will be forgiven in exchange for the daughter's hand in marriage.

Both the merchant and his daughter are understandably horrified. The moneylender, however, devises a seemingly inescapable dilemma. He proposes a "lucky pick" – placing a black and a white pebble in a bag. The daughter must pick one. If she chooses black, she becomes his wife, and the debt is cleared. Picking white grants her freedom from marriage, and the debt is still forgiven. Refusal to pick a pebble results in the father's imprisonment.

They stand in the merchant's garden, on a path strewn with pebbles. The situation appears hopeless. Three options present themselves: refuse and face imprisonment, expose the cheat (meaning the debt remains), or sacrifice herself. However, the daughter demonstrates remarkable resourcefulness.

With a quick mind, she reaches into the bag, retrieves a pebble, and – fumbling – drops it onto the path where it disappears among the countless others. "How clumsy of me!" she exclaims. "But no matter, if you simply look in the bag for the remaining pebble, you'll know which one I picked."

The moneylender is caught in his own web. Since the remaining pebble is black, it implies she must have chosen the white one. Unable to expose his own deceit by revealing the black pebble, he is forced to concede defeat. The daughter's cleverness transforms an impossible situation into a victory.

Adapted from various versions on the internet.

Ponder this:

This story reminds us that even the most challenging problems can be overcome with a dash of ingenuity. Sometimes, the key lies in approaching the situation from a different angle, questioning assumptions, and using our wit to find a solution that may not be immediately obvious.

The Parable of the Twin Fetuses

Once upon a time, a woman conceived twin boys. Nestled within their mother's womb, they celebrated their existence.

They explored their world, marveled at the life-giving cord, and sang praises to their unseen mother: "How great our mother's love is, that she shares her own life with us!"

As time passed, the twins noticed how much each was changing.

The weeks stretched into months, their awareness grew, and so did their anxieties. One twin, filled with apprehension, questioned the inevitable change.

"What happens after?" he asked. "I don't want to leave this world; I want to stay here always," he added.

The other, more optimistic, offered a glimmer of hope. "Perhaps there's life beyond this place."

But the first twin clung to pessimism. "How can there be? We rely on the cord. Without it, how can we survive? Besides, we have seen evidence that others were here before us, and none of them has returned. Surely this is the end."

"But who created us?" the optimist countered. "And how do we exist now? There must be a mother, a source for all this."

The pessimist, however, remained unconvinced. "Have we ever seen her? Maybe she only lives in our minds. Perhaps she's just a comforting illusion."

Doubt and fear filled their final days in the womb.

Finally, the moment of birth arrived. Thrust into a new world, they opened their eyes, not to darkness, but to a dazzling spectacle beyond their wildest dreams. They cried – tears not of fear, but of overwhelming joy.

Adapted from various versions on the internet.

Ponder this:

This parable beautifully captures the human tendency to resist change. The unknown can be frightening, yet it often holds possibilities far exceeding our limited imaginations. Just like the twins, we must embrace change with an open mind and a hopeful heart. The greatest experiences may lie just beyond the familiar.

The Devil's Best Tool

One day, the devil decided that God had received too much good publicity and he too deserved some acknowledgment for the work he does to make this world an interesting place. He called a major TV news network and, after identifying himself, arranged an interview.

For the interview, he transported the reporter and the camera crew to Hell and gave them a tour of a strange sort of art gallery. His gallery did not consist of elements of great art. Instead, his gallery was made up of a number of rooms of varying sizes, each one dedicated to a specific item of interest. In one room were piles of gold on a marble table, stacked to the ceiling. "This is my greed room," the devil said. "Greed is one of my favorite tools."

Moving to the second room, the devil showed the reporter and camera crew a group of men and women enjoying themselves in a cocktail lounge at a convention. "This is my infidelity room," the devil said. "This is a place of temptation for those who are far away from home."

The devil continued in this manner, proudly presenting rooms with addictive drugs, alcohol, firearms, weapons, and other destructive items.

Finally, the camera crew came to the last room. The devil paused and said, "Herein lies my greatest tool. With this tool, I can accomplish more evil than with all the other tools at my disposal, put together."

Keen to see the contents of this room, the camera crew and the reporter moved closer to the door as the devil opened it triumphantly. In the room was a small item on a pedestal illuminated by a spotlight.

At first glance, it appeared to be a seemingly harmless wedge-shaped object. Curiously, the camera crew edged closer to the object, only to find that it was a simple wedge – similar to a common doorstop.

Bewildered by how this could be his greatest tool, they turned and looked at the devil inquiringly, as if to ask, "What in 'hell' is this?"

"This," the devil smilingly revealed, "is the wedge of self-doubt. With it, I can shatter a person's self-image. I drive this wedge into the back of a person's mind between their abilities and potential. If I create a gap between someone's abilities and what is truly possible for them, then I can literally destroy that person. It is worn down so much because I use it with nearly everybody. "

Indeed, even a flicker of doubt can paralyze and prevent individuals from achieving their full potential. This, the devil concluded, is what truly hinders most people from leading better lives.

Adapted from various versions on the internet.

Ponder this:

The story emphasizes the insidious power of self-doubt as a barrier to personal growth and achievement. Many of us have tiny cracks in our self-image and when we allow ourselves or other people to drive the 'wedge of doubt' into those cracks, we set ourselves up for catastrophic failure.

A True Story ("Trying Harder")

I'm sitting in a quiet room at the Millcroft Inn, a peaceful little place hidden back among the pine trees about an hour out of Toronto. It's just past noon, late July, and I'm listening to the desperate sounds of a life-or-death struggle going on a few feet away.

There's a small fly burning out the last of its short life's energies in a futile attempt to fly through the glass of the windowpane. The whining wings tell the poignant story of the fly's strategy – try harder.

But it's not working.

The frenzied effort offers no hope for survival. Ironically, the struggle is part of the trap. It is impossible for the fly to try hard enough to succeed at breaking through the glass. Nevertheless, this little insect has staked its life on reaching its goal through raw effort and determination.

This fly is doomed. It will die there on the windowsill.

Across the room, ten steps away, the door is open. Ten seconds of flying time and this small creature could reach the outside world it seeks. With only a fraction of the effort now being wasted, it could be free of this self-imposed trap. The breakthrough possibility is there. It would be so easy.

Why doesn't the fly try another approach, something dramatically different? How did it get so locked in on the idea that this particular route, and determined effort, offer the most promise for success? What logic is there in continuing, until death, to seek a breakthrough with "more of the same"?

No doubt this approach makes sense to the fly. Regrettably, it's an idea that will kill.

"Trying harder" isn't necessarily the solution to achieving more. It may not offer any real promise for getting what you want out of life. Sometimes, in fact, it's a big part of the problem.

If you stake your hopes for a breakthrough on trying harder than ever, you may kill your chances for success.

(Pritchett, 2012)

Ponder this:

If a strategy isn't working – if you're stuck – "trying harder" is rarely the answer. Instead, come up with a new plan! Step back, study the situation from a new angle, and rethink your assumptions. Breakthroughs come when you "try differently."

Lessons Learnt In (Re)Morse Code

Back when the telegraph was the fastest method of long-distance communication, a young man applied for a job as a Morse code operator.

Answering an advertisement in the newspaper, he went to the office address listed. He entered a large, busy office filled with noise and clatter including the sound of the telegraph in the background. A sign on the receptionist's counter instructed job applicants to fill out a form and wait until summoned to enter the Manager's office.

The young man filled out his form and sat down with the seven other applicants in the waiting area. After a few minutes, he stood up, crossed the room to the manager's office and walked right in. Naturally, the other applicants perked up, wondering what was going on. They muttered among themselves that they hadn't heard any summons yet. They assumed that the young man who had gone into the office had made a mistake, and he would be ineligible.

Within a few minutes, however, the manager escorted the young man out of the office and said to the other applicants, "Gentleman, thank you very much for coming. The job has now been filled."

The other applicants began grumbling to each other, and one spoke up saying, "Wait a minute, I don't understand! He was the last to come in, and we never got a chance to be interviewed. Yet he got the job. That's not fair!"

The manager said, "I'm sorry, but all the time you've been sitting here, the telegraph has been ticking out the following message in Morse code: 'If you understand this message, then come right in.

The job is yours.' None of you listened carefully or understood it. This young man did. The job is his."

Adapted from various versions on the internet.

Ponder this:

The parable teaches us that we should pay attention to details and not make assumptions. Just like the young man who listened carefully to the Morse code message, we should be alert and attentive to the opportunities that come our way. By doing so, we can seize the moment and achieve success.

The Lady or the Tiger?

In a distant kingdom ruled by a semi-barbaric king, justice takes an unconventional form. Instead of gladiator battles or executions, the king conducts criminal trials in an amphitheatre. This unique trial involves two doors: one concealing a ferocious tiger, and the other, a beautiful lady. When an accused man enters the amphitheatre, he must choose a door. If he picks the tiger, he meets a gruesome end, confirming his guilt. If he selects the lady, he is immediately married to her, regardless of his existing marital status.

The Scandal and the Princess's Dilemma
The plot thickens when the king's daughter, secretly in love with a young man of low social standing, becomes embroiled in a scandal. The king discovers their affair and demands the usual trial for her lover. This time, the stakes are higher: the most ferocious tiger awaits behind one door, while the most beautiful lady in the kingdom stands behind the other [door].

The Princess's Jealousy
The princess knows which door hides the tiger and which holds the lady. She despises the lady, who happens to be someone from the king's court and has feelings for the young man. Consumed by jealousy, the princess imagines the woman eagerly awaiting her marriage to the young man. Her heart torn between love and possessiveness; she must make a fateful decision.

The Trial and the Uncertain Outcome
As the young man enters the amphitheatre, he bows respectfully to the king. His eyes seek the princess, suspecting she knows which door leads to which fate. In a quick gesture, she signals him to choose the right door.

The young man, trusting the princess with his life, confidently strides towards the indicated door. But it is not known which fate the princess has chosen for him.

The Unresolved Ending

The story ends without revealing whether the lady or the tiger emerges. Instead, we are left with lingering questions:

- Did the princess help him to escape the fate of the tiger's jaws, and effectively give the man she loves to another woman, condemning herself to heartbreak?
- Or did her jealousy get the better of her, and she gestured to the door behind which the tiger waits to devour him to prevent him from marrying a woman she despises?

Effectively, the readers of this story are the final 'authors' of the story's conclusion.

(Adapted from Stockton, 1882)

Ponder this:

The author masterfully leaves the conclusion open-ended, causing us to wonder about the outcome. In essence, "The Lady, or the Tiger?" invites us to reflect on our own choices, emotions, and the unpredictable nature of existence.

Whether the young man faces the tiger or the lady, fate plays a significant role. Sometimes, despite our intentions, external factors shape our lives. We learn that consequences are often beyond our control.

To Be Successful, Burn Your Boats

The story of Hernán Cortés and his conquest of the Aztec empire is a classic example of the “burning boats” concept. At its essence, burning boats represents a point of no return, a psychological commitment where you recognize that you have crossed a line never to cross back.

In 1519, Cortés led a large expedition consisting of 600 Spaniards, 16 or so horses, and 11 boats to Mexico. The goal: capture a magnificent treasure said to be held there.

Upon arrival, Cortés made history by destroying his ships that had carried them there.

Motivating his men before the battle, Cortés said, pointing at the burning ships, “you see the boats going up in smoke. That means that we cannot leave these shores alive unless we win! We now have no choice – we win or we perish.”

Although you might assume that Cortés’ men would have become despondent, with no exit strategy in place to save their lives, they instead rallied behind their leader as never before.

By destroying their own means of retreat, Cortés and his men were forced to give their all in the battle. They had no option but to fight with unwavering resolve, knowing that victory was their only path to survival.

Within two years, he succeeded in his conquest of the Aztec empire.

(Some date this concept of “burning boats” even further back in history, to the times of Julius Caesar – in his conquest of England – or even the Ancient Greeks. Regardless, the scenarios and impact were similar.)

(Adapted from Hoff, 2017)

Ponder this:

The story teaches us that real success often means going all-in and not having a backup plan. When you're faced with a big challenge that feels impossible, don't give yourself an easy way out. If something really matters to you, you'll do whatever it takes to make it happen. But if you have a Plan B that's easier, you might not push yourself to do the hard work needed for true success.

Now, does this mean that just wanting to win will guarantee victory? Not exactly. But it does mean that without a lot of passion and determination, success is pretty hard to reach. So, when you're chasing your dreams, give it your all and don't hold back!

It's a Crow: A Lesson in Empathy

An elderly father and his middle-aged son sat on the living room couch. A crow landed on their windowsill.

"What is that?" the father inquired.

"It's a crow, Dad," replied the son.

A few minutes later, the father asked again: "What is that?"

"Father, I just told you, it's a crow," the son answered, a hint of impatience in his voice.

A little while later, the elderly father asked his son again: "What is that?"

"A crow, I said," the son repeated, with a distinct annoyance in his tone.

Shortly after, the forgetful father questioned his son once more: "What is that?"

"Why do you keep asking the same thing?" the son finally shouted. "Can't you understand, IT'S A CROW!"

Confused and hurt, the father retreated to his room, returning with a worn journal filled with memories from their past. He asked his son to read a particular entry.

The son's eyes scanned the faded words: "Today, my son, just three years old, curiously asked 'What is that?' twenty-three times when a crow landed on our windowsill. Each time, I answered 'It's a crow,' without a single moment of annoyance. Instead, with every question, I embraced him, expressing love for my inquisitive child."

The journal's inscription hit the son like a revelation. His father patiently answered the same question twenty-three times, but he couldn't tolerate even four repetitions now. The realization left him speechless.

Adapted from various versions on the internet.

Ponder this:

The roles of caregiver and dependant often reverse as people age. The story encourages us to cultivate patience and empathy in our interactions with others, especially when dealing with repeated questions or concerning behaviours from aging loved ones.

A Student's Quest for Success

A student, eager for a shortcut to success, approached his spiritual teacher for guidance. The teacher smiled knowingly and instructed, "Meet me at the Ganges River at 5:00 am tomorrow."

Intrigued, the student arrived on time, finding his teacher wading in the river, beckoning him to join. Wanting to uncover the secret to success, the student complied.

Suddenly, the teacher submerged the student's head underwater. Gasping for air, the student struggled, panicking. The teacher held him down for what felt like an eternity before finally releasing him.

Sputtering, the student demanded, "Why did you do that?"

The calm teacher responded, "While you were underwater, what consumed your thoughts? Success? Wealth? Recognition?"

The student, catching his breath, replied, "No, sir. All I craved was air. Nothing but air."

The teacher's message was clear: "If you desire success with the same relentless intensity that you desired that breath of air, success will be yours. It will come to you as swiftly as you desire."

Adapted from various versions on the internet.

Ponder this:

This story isn't about recklessness or blind ambition; it's about the intensity of desire. The student's actions reflected a lukewarm ambition. The teacher suggests that true success demands an all-consuming drive, a relentless pursuit that mirrors the desperate need for air. So, think about it: do your everyday actions reflect a burning desire for your goals, or are they half-hearted attempts? Only an unshakeable hunger for success will endure the relentless effort required to achieve it.

The Real Meaning of Peace

There once was a king who offered a prize to the artist who would paint the best picture of peace. The contest stirred the imagination of artists everywhere. Many artists wanted a chance at winning the prize. Paintings from far and wide began to arrive.

The king looked at all the pictures, uncovering one peaceful scene after another as the on-lookers clapped and cheered. The tensions grew as only two pictures remained veiled. As the king pulled the cover from one, a hush fell over the crowd.

It was a picture of a calm lake. The lake was a perfect mirror for peaceful towering mountains all around it. Overhead was a beautiful blue sky with fluffy white clouds. Along the grassy shore, a flock of sheep grazed undisturbed. All who saw this picture thought that it was a perfect picture of peace. Surely this was the winner.

The king uncovered the last painting, and the crowd gasped in surprise. Could this be peace? This picture had mountains like the previous painting but these were rugged and bare. Above was an angry sky, from which rain fell and in which lightning played. Down the side of the mountain tumbled a foaming waterfall; the crowd could almost feel its cold, penetrating spray. This did not look peaceful at all.

But, when the king looked closely, he saw that behind the waterfall was a tiny bush growing in the rock. Inside the bush, a mother bird had built her nest. There, in the midst of the rush of angry water, sat the mother bird on her nest.

She was the perfect picture of peace.

The king chose the second picture.

Adapted from (Coelho, 2003)

Ponder this:

The story of the king and the two paintings offers a profound perspective on peace. Instead of just thinking of peace as a serene environment with no problems, it challenges us to see it as something inside us, no matter what's happening outside. Life has its calm moments and stormy times, and wanting everything to be perfect all the time isn't realistic and can even inhibit our personal growth.

The real challenge is finding inner peace even when everything around us is chaotic. The mother bird, nestled in the heart of the storm, embodies this concept beautifully. Her unflinching composure, amidst the fury of the waterfall, represents our capacity for inner serenity, even when the world around us feels anything but peaceful.

This story teaches us to be strong and resilient. It shows that true peace isn't about having no problems but about staying calm and composed even when things get tough. When we find peace within ourselves, we equip ourselves to weather life's inevitable storms and come out stronger on the other side. This deeper understanding of peace is the significant lesson from the story.

The Tunnel

Zenkai, the son of a samurai, journeyed to Edo and there became the retainer of a high official. He fell in love with the official's wife and was discovered. In self-defence, he slew the official. Then he ran away with his wife.

Both of them later became thieves. But the woman was so greedy that Zenkai grew disgusted. Finally, leaving her, he journeyed far away to the province of Buzen, where he became a wandering mendicant.

To atone for his past, Zenkai resolved to accomplish some good deed in his lifetime. Knowing of a dangerous road over a cliff that had caused the death and injury of many persons, he resolved to cut a tunnel through the mountain there.

Begging food in the daytime, Zenkai worked at night digging his tunnel. When thirty years had gone by, the tunnel was 2,280 feet long, 20 feet high, and 30 feet wide.

Two years before the work was completed, the son of the official he had slain, who was a skilful swordsman, found Zenkai out and came to kill him in revenge.

"I will give you my life willingly," said Zenkai. "Only let me finish this work. On the day it is completed, then you may kill me."

So the son awaited the day. Several months passed and Zenkai kept on digging. The son grew tired of doing nothing and began to help with the digging. After he had helped for more than a year, he came to admire Zenkai's strong will and character.

At last the tunnel was completed and the people could use it and travel in safety.

"Now cut off my head," said Zenkai. "My work is done."

"How can I cut off my own teacher's head?" asked the younger man with tears in his eyes.

Adapted from various versions on the internet.

Ponder this:

The story teaches us that it's never too late to make amends for our past mistakes and that even the most heinous of sins can be redeemed through hard work and dedication to a noble cause.

Challenges Make Us Stronger

Life throws difficulties our way – it's inevitable. But believe it or not, most of these problems can actually benefit us! Let me explain.

The Great Barrier Reef, a magnificent coral reef system stretching 1,800 miles from New Guinea to Australia, is a popular tourist destination. On one particular tour, a visitor noticed a curious difference between the lagoon and ocean sides of the reef. "The lagoon coral appears pale and lifeless," they remarked, "while the ocean coral is vibrant and colorful. Why the difference?"

The guide's answer was insightful. "The lagoon's still waters present no challenge to the coral's survival. It stagnates and dies young. In contrast, the ocean side endures constant testing by wind, waves, and storms. This fight for survival forces the coral to adapt and grow stronger, healthier, and more capable of reproduction." He added a thought-provoking conclusion: "That's how it is with all living things."

The same principle applies to humans. We thrive on challenges. Just like the coral battered by the sea, we grow from the experiences that test us. Physical demands increase our strength, mental and emotional stresses build resilience, and spiritual trials cultivate character and faith.

So, next time you face a difficulty, don't despair! See it as an opportunity for growth. Tell yourself, "Here I grow again!"

Adapted from various versions on the internet.

Ponder this:

The story uses the coral as a metaphor to show how, like coral, people can thrive in the face of adversity. A challenging environment isn't simply a hardship; it's a catalyst for growth and development. When we embrace life's challenges, we build resilience, gain strength, and find more meaning in what we do. Just as the vibrant coral thrives in the face of adversity, we too can weather the storms of life and emerge stronger and more amazing.

The Pike Fish Experiment

A pike fish was once put in a tank along with many small minnows. The pike wasted no time eating all the minnows.

The next day, a glass partition was placed into the tank dividing the tank in two. At feeding time, instead of putting the live minnows in with the pike, the minnows were placed on the other side of the partition. The pike could see the minnows but could not get to them. Unable to detect the glass divider, the pike repeatedly slammed its head against it in pursuit of its meal. After countless failed attempts, it gave up entirely.

Days later, the glass partition was removed from the tank allowing the pike to swim freely amongst the minnows. It could now easily eat the minnows, but the strangest thing happened. Even though the pike hadn't eaten in days and the minnows were within easy reach, it made no attempt to hunt. The relentless frustration of its prior attempts had sapped its will to hunt. Surrounded by food, the pike perished.

Adapted from various versions on the internet.

Ponder this:

The plight of the pike provides a sobering analogy to human behavior. We humans become conditioned in much the same way as other creatures. If we keep failing, we begin to believe we are incapable of success and, sooner or later, we just stop trying.

This story emphasizes the importance of maintaining a positive mindset, even in the face of adversity. By reframing failure as a learning experience and trusting in our own abilities, we can overcome challenges and achieve our goals.

Lessons from Geese

When you see geese heading south for the winter, they fly in a V formation. Science has discovered why they fly that way. The following exposition is by Dr Robert McNish (a former science teacher).

- Research has revealed that as each bird flaps its wings, it creates an up lift for the bird immediately behind it. By flying in a V formation, the whole flock adds at least 71% greater flying range than if each bird flew on its own. (*People who share a common direction and sense of community get where they are going more quickly and easily because they are traveling on one another's thrust.*)
- Whenever a goose falls out of formation, it suddenly feels the drag and resistance of trying to go it alone. It quickly gets back into formation to take advantage of the lifting power of the bird immediately in front. (*If we have as much sense as a goose, we will stay in formation and with those who are headed the same way we are.*)
- When the lead goose gets tired, he rotates back in the V and another goose flies the point. (*It pays to take turns doing the hard jobs. As with geese, people are interdependent of each other's skills, capabilities, talents or resources.*)
- The geese honk from behind to encourage those up front to keep up their speed. (*Likewise, we need to make sure our honking is encouraging, not discouraging. In groups where there is encouragement, production is much greater.*)
- Finally, when a goose gets sick or is wounded by gunfire and falls out, two other geese fall out of formation and follow it down to help and protect it. They stay with the incapacitated goose until it is either able to fly again or dies. Only then will they launch out on their own or with another formation to

catch up with their group. (*If we have the sense of a goose, we will stand by each other in times of need.*)

(Widemark, 2009)

Ponder this:

The lessons learned from observing geese offers valuable insights into building a successful life. By embracing collaboration, shared leadership, encouragement, and genuine support, we can create powerful synergies that drive each other toward success. Remember, we are not meant to navigate life's journey alone. When we team up and create a strong sense of community, we can achieve way more than if we try to do everything by ourselves. So, let's learn from the geese and use teamwork and community to reach our goals and soar to new heights!

The Power of an Emotive Affirmation

Every human thought, word or deed is a cause that sets off a wave of energy throughout the universe, resulting in desirable or undesirable effects. If there are undesirable effects, it simply means that at some time in the past, there was a thought, word or deed that caused a wave of undesirable energy. As normal, fully-functioning people we are quite literally responsible for everything in our lives. The following excerpt illustrates this concept.

This is the suggestion a man gave to his subconscious mind over a period of about two years: "I would give my right arm to see my daughter cured." It appeared that his daughter had a crippling form of arthritis together with a so-called incurable form of skin disease. Medical treatment had failed to alleviate the condition, and the father had an intense longing for his daughter's healing, and expressed his desire in the words just quoted.

One day the family was out for a drive. Their car was involved in a head-on collision. The father's right arm was torn off at the shoulder. When he came home from the hospital, he discovered that his daughter's arthritis and skin condition had vanished.

(Murphy, 2001)

Ponder this:

The story teaches us a valuable lesson about how our thoughts and wishes can have unexpected consequences. While the father's intention was pure – a desperate longing for his daughter's well-being – his subconscious mind interpreted his words literally, leading to a tragic outcome. It reminds us to be careful with what we wish for and how we think about things. Instead of dwelling on what we're willing to sacrifice, it's better to focus on the positive outcome we want.

The Weight of the Glass

Once upon a time, a psychology professor was teaching stress management principles to an auditorium full of students. As she walked around the stage, she raised a glass of water. Everyone expected the typical "glass half empty or glass half full" question. Instead, with a smile, the professor asked, "How heavy is this glass of water I'm holding?"

Students shouted out answers ranging from eight ounces to a couple of pounds.

She replied, "From my perspective, the absolute weight of this glass doesn't matter. It all depends on how long I hold it. If I hold it for a minute or two, it's fairly light. If I hold it for an hour straight, its weight might make my arm ache a little. If I hold it for a day straight, my arm will likely cramp up and feel completely numb and paralyzed, forcing me to drop the glass to the floor. In each case, the weight of the glass doesn't change, but the longer I hold it, the heavier it feels to me."

As the class nodded in agreement, she continued, "Your stresses and worries in life are very much like this glass of water. Think about them for a while, and nothing happens. Think about them a bit longer, and you begin to ache a little. Think about them all day long, and you will feel completely numb and paralyzed – incapable of doing anything else until you drop them."

Likewise, it's important to remember to let go of your stresses and worries. No matter what happens during the day, put all your burdens down as early in the evening as you can. Don't carry them through the night and into the next day with you. If you still feel the weight of yesterday's stress, it's a strong sign that it's time to put the glass down.

Adapted from various versions on the internet.

Ponder this:

The professor's analogy of the glass of water is an excellent example of how our perception of stress can change over time. Just like the weight of the glass feels heavier the longer we hold it, worrying too much can make our burdens feel overwhelming.

The story reminds us that stress isn't just a mental burden; it can show physically as well. Chronic stress can lead to headaches, muscle tension, and even fatigue. The lesson here is to not let stress pile up until it's too much to handle.

By consciously letting go of worries, similar to putting down the glass, we can prevent them from accumulating and impacting our well-being. The story inspires us to find healthy ways to cope, like staying active, eating well, and practicing mindfulness. When we learn to handle stress this way, we can feel more at peace and handle whatever life throws our way with strength.

Two Frogs in Trouble

One sunny day, Big Frog and Little Frog were hopping along when they accidentally tumbled into a bucket of fresh milk. Panic set in as they realized the sides were too slippery to climb. They began paddling frantically, trying to stay afloat.

Their fellow frogs gathered around the bucket, watching the spectacle. Instead of offering encouragement, they shouted discouraging words: “It’s hopeless! Why bother? Just give up!”

As time passed, Big Frog grew tired. The constant paddling and the negative comments wore him down. “What’s the point?” he sighed, giving in to despair. He stopped paddling and sank to the bottom.

But Little Frog wasn’t ready to quit. Ignoring the taunts, he focused on survival. He kept paddling, determined to overcome this challenge.

As the hours ticked by, the milk began to thicken, making it harder to swim. Little Frog’s legs were almost paralyzed with exhaustion. It seemed like he couldn’t last much longer. But a thought kept him going: “Giving up is like being dead. I’ll keep swimming as long as I can. While there’s life, there’s hope.”

With renewed determination, Little Frog churned the milk into waves. Just when he thought all hope was lost, he felt something solid beneath his feet. To his amazement, his constant paddling had churned the milk into butter! He leaped onto this self-made platform and out of the bucket to freedom.

Now, you might think the difference between Little Frog and Big Frog was simply that Little Frog had more heart and more determination. And you’d be partly right. But there was another crucial difference – Little Frog was deaf. He couldn’t hear the discouraging words from the other frogs. In fact, he thought they were cheering him on: "Keep going, Little Frog! You can do it!"

Adapted from various versions on the internet.

Ponder this:

This story teaches us a powerful lesson: persistence is the key to success. But it also shows us the importance of our mindset. Even when faced with negativity, focusing on encouragement – whether it's real or something we create in our minds – can fuel our perseverance and lead us to success.

Remember this profound truth: The Universe only fully releases her rewards *after* you refuse to quit!

Your "Mystical" Mind

Claire, a former professional dancer, was 47 and dying from a disease called primary pulmonary hypertension when, in 1988, she had a pioneering heart-lung transplant in America. After she recovered from the operation, she suddenly had a craving for beer and KFC (Kentucky Fried Chicken). She was baffled because she had never before desired either. According to her teenage daughter, she even began walking like a man.

Months after the operation, she began having mysterious dreams about a young man named Tim. She tracked down the donor of her new organs and learnt that they had come from Timothy, the victim of a fatal motorcycle accident. When she contacted his family, the woman was stunned to discover that he did have a particular fondness for drinking beer and eating KFC.

(Sylvia, 2008)

Ponder this:

Claire's story is undeniably intriguing. It raises the question: Is information stored in every cell of our body and not only in the brain or mind?

While the idea of cellular memory – information is stored within every cell – is a captivating one, scientific evidence for such a phenomenon remains inconclusive. A more likely explanation for Claire's experience lies in the complex interplay between the immune system and the brain. Claire's story highlights the fascinating mysteries surrounding the connections between body and mind. It reveals the body's remarkable ability to adapt and the intricate communication pathways that exist within us.

The Crab Bucket

A man walking along the beach came across a fisherman with a bucket of crabs beside him. Noticing the bucket wasn't covered, the man asked the fisherman why he didn't secure the crabs to stop them from escaping. The fisherman explained, "Crabs have a 'mass mentality.' If there's only one crab in the bucket, it will quickly climb out. But when there are many crabs, if one tries to climb up, the others grab it and pull it back down so that it shares their fate."

Adapted from various versions on the internet.

Ponder this:

This short story vividly illustrates a common human behavior: holding others back out of jealousy or fear. It's like crabs in a bucket trying to stop one another from escaping. When someone strives to improve their situation, pursue a dream, or simply break free from the ordinary, they may encounter a surprising resistance. Others, stuck in their own routines or insecurities, might attempt to belittle their efforts or block their progress.

The story is a reminder to watch out for those who try to squash your dreams. Stay brave and focused on your goals, and don't let jealous behavior discourage you from reaching for more.

A Cherokee Parable

An elderly Cherokee Native American was teaching his grandchildren about life.

He said to them, "A fight is going on inside me, it is a terrible fight and it is between two wolves. One wolf is evil – he is fear, anger, rage, envy, sorrow, regret, greed, arrogance, self-pity, guilt, resentment, inferiority, lies, false pride, competition, superiority, and ego.

The other is good – he is love, joy, greatness, peace, hope, sharing, serenity, humility, kindness, benevolence, friendship, empathy, generosity, truth, compassion and faith.

This same fight is going on inside you, and inside every other person, too."

They thought about it for a minute, and then one child asked his grandfather, "Which wolf will win, Grandfather?"

The elder simply replied, "The one you feed."

Adapted from various versions on the internet.

Ponder this:

This story does not stop at merely separating good from evil – it's about the two traits (or capacities) we all have inside us. The key message lies in the grandfather's response: "The one you feed." They show how important our choices are. When we focus on the good stuff like love and kindness, it grows stronger and guides us in positive ways. But if we let negativity take over, it can get a grip on us. The story reminds us that we're not powerless bystanders in this inner struggle; we have the power to decide which side wins.

Perspective:
It's Funny How Things Change

Dr Norman Vincent Peale, an Ohio-born preacher and author of the mega-bestseller, The Power of Positive Thinking, tells a story of a man who phoned him one day, deeply depressed and looking for help. Peale invited the man to his office for a chat, during which the man told him he had nothing to live for anymore.

"Everything is gone, hopeless," the man told him. "I'm living in deepest darkness. In fact, I've lost heart for living altogether."

Peale smiled sympathetically at the distraught man sitting before him. "Let's take a look at your situation," he said, taking out a sheet of paper and drawing a line down the middle of the paper. He told the man on the left side they would list the things he'd lost in his life, and on the right, the things he had remaining.

"You won't need that column on the right side," said the man sadly. "I have nothing left, period."

Peale asked, "When did your wife leave you?"

"What do you mean? She hasn't left me. My wife loves me!"

"That's great!" said Peale enthusiastically. "Then that will be number one in the right-hand column – Wife hasn't left. Now, when were your children jailed?"

"What?" the man asked, surprised. "My children aren't in jail!"

"Good! That's number two in the right-hand column – Children not in jail," said Peale, jotting it down.

After a few more questions in the same vein, the man finally got the point and smiled in spite of himself. "Funny, how things change when you think of them that way," he said.

Adapted from various versions on the internet.

Ponder this:

Dr. Peale's story serves as a powerful reminder about the transformative power of perspective. When consumed by negativity, we often lose sight of the blessings still present in our lives. By simply shifting our focus to what we haven't lost, the story reminds us that even in challenging times, there are always reasons for gratitude. The act of listing these positives, as Dr. Peale suggests, can be a powerful tool for combating negativity and fostering a more optimistic outlook.

Dr. Wayne Dyer famously said, "when we change the way we look at things, the things we look at change." Sit with that quote for a moment!

The Story of the Pencil

A curious grandson observes his grandmother writing a letter and asks if the story is about him. The grandmother, however, reveals a deeper purpose.

She describes the pencil as more significant than the words themselves. This piques the grandson's curiosity, prompting her to unveil five valuable qualities that the pencil embodies – qualities that she hopes her grandson will embrace to develop a strong personal character.

The First Quality: Recognizing a Higher Power. The first quality highlights the importance of acknowledging a guiding force in our lives. The pencil, though capable of great things, relies on a hand to direct it. Similarly, we are guided by a higher power, a force for good that shapes our path.

The Second Quality: Embracing Challenges. The second quality emphasizes the necessity of enduring hardship. Just as a pencil is sharpened to become a better tool, we too must learn to endure difficulties, as they ultimately refine our character and resilience.

The Third Quality: Learning from Mistakes. The eraser on the pencil signifies the importance of acknowledging and correcting our mistakes. This willingness to learn and adapt paves the way for growth and self-improvement.

The Fourth Quality: Focusing on Inner Worth. The true value of the pencil lies not in its outer shell but in the graphite within. The core of the pencil, the graphite, represents our inner selves. It emphasizes the importance of nurturing our values, beliefs, and morals, as these form the foundation of who we are.

The Fifth Quality: Leaving a Positive Mark. The pencil leaves a mark with every stroke, and so do we. Our actions, big or small, have consequences. This awareness encourages us to strive to create a positive impact throughout our lives.

Adapted from (Coelho, 2009)

Ponder this:

This story transcends the pencil's simplicity. It conveys a timeless message about the potential for greatness within each of us. By embracing these core values, we can grow into well-rounded individuals who make a positive impact on the world around us.

Advice for Couples – Be like the Cashew Nut and not like the Walnut

As I wait for our 50th marriage anniversary in a few months' time, I look back at the past with nostalgia, revel in the present with wonder and look forward to the future with anticipation.

What advice can I give those couples who are looking forward to their own 50th anniversary in, maybe, 49 years? Or even in one year?

Based on my experience, I would like to tell all couples living together – married or not – that, if you want a fulfilling life, be like the Cashew nut and not the Walnut.

Let me explain.

The Walnut comprises two halves, separated by a gap called the shell seal. In this gap there is a thin but strong membrane, keeping the two halves from touching each other.

The two halves are connected at just one point. For couples who live as Walnuts, this point of connection can be sex, children, the perceived sanctity of wedding vows, family pressure or something else. Their interests join at this point. At all other places, they are separated by this membrane occupying the shell seal. Thus, there is no connection at other points and the two live their separate inner – and often, outer – lives without meaningful interaction with each other except at the connection point.

The connection point can make living together last long but such a union is an unhappy one and is usually full of silent, but sometimes, voluble, desperation. The couple is together and not yet together. Sometimes this kind of unhappy existence is not acceptable and the union ends in separation with the connecting point broken. Where children or property are involved, this broken connection point can become a contentious issue.

The two halves of the Cashew nut, on the other hand, stay close together at all points, harmoniously nestling against each other. Their connection at one point is stronger than at other points but the other points are not ignored and there is communication between them at diverse places on the surfaces where they meet.

Despite extensive communication with each other, we must remember that the two halves of a Cashew nut do not merge into each other. In ideal togetherness, they remain their own selves and continue to keep their individual identities intact.

I urge you to review your interaction with your other half. If you find that it is more Walnut-like, it is never too late to change it. Unlike in the case of the actual Walnut and the Cashew nut, sincere effort on both sides can change the reality from one to the other in the case of relationships.

A sincere wish for making things better, an open heart combined with mutual kindness and consideration can work wonders. A recognition that good relationships are more about giving than receiving make the transition smoother. For some this may also require asking their ego to shut up and take a back seat.

Sadly, sometimes this works the other way around, too. A Cashew nut like union metamorphoses into Walnut mode. A shell space develops between the couple, separating the two. This could be formed by interference by other relatives or friends, over-preoccupation with children, extra-marital interests or just plain boredom with each other. Sometimes this could be illness, depression or other psychological issues. A partnership that was going well earlier thus becomes Walnut like.

This fate can be avoided if close attention is paid to the shell seal membrane as it develops. If checked at the correct time, it can be dissolved and the togetherness that was there earlier can be reinstated. Unfortunately, this separating membrane develops insidiously and is usually taken for granted during the initial stages. It then acquires thickness and strength before the couple realizes what is happening and gradually, they segue into the Walnut mode.

When this happens, sometimes, in introspective moments, one or the other fruitlessly wonders what happened to their paradise-that-was.

One last point – remember, both the Cashew nut and the Walnut are seeds. Their progeny will grow as per their own nature. Their children will tend to remember and emulate what they have seen at home. The progeny of a Walnut is more likely to become a Walnut and the progeny of a Cashew nut more likely to become a Cashew nut. This is not always true though. Much also depends upon their other halves but if both halves come from similar seeds, it won't be surprising if they grow into similar fruit.

In conclusion, I would like to reiterate – watch closely what your relationship with your other half resembles. If it is more like a Walnut, try to change it akin to a Cashew nut. If it is like a Cashew nut, guard it with all your mental and physical resources for there can be nothing more precious, in terms of relationships, than a fulfilling togetherness.

~ Kishore Asthana (kishore.asthana@gmail.com)

Ponder this:

The author suggests that couples who are like cashews, with multiple points of connection, are more likely to have a fulfilling life together, and every relationship should want to achieve that. It is a simple yet powerful message that can help couples strengthen their bonds.

Eyes 'Slant'

A prominent Chinese came to America to be educated in American ways. He attended the University of Chicago.

One day President Harper met this young Oriental on the campus, stopped to chat with him for a few minutes, and asked what had impressed him as being the most noticeable characteristic of the American people.

"Why," the Chinaman exclaimed, "the queer slant of your eyes. Your eyes are off slant!"

What do we say about the Chinese? We refuse to believe that which we do not understand. We foolishly believe that our own limitations are the proper measure of limitations. Sure, the other fellow's eyes are "off slant," *because they are not the same as our own.*

(Hill, 2014)

Ponder this:

The "slant" of the eyes serves as a powerful reminder of our tendency to perceive things as strange or wrong when they differ from our own norms. This story reminds us to stay open-minded. Our own experiences shape how we see the world, but they shouldn't close us off from other ways of thinking. If we recognize that our view isn't the only one and try to understand others' experiences and viewpoints, we can learn to empathize and connect with people from different backgrounds.

The Burnt Biscuit

As a child, the aroma of breakfast for dinner always held a special allure. Yet, one evening, amidst the hustle and bustle of our home, my mother embarked on a culinary endeavor after a taxing day's work.

I can vividly recall the scene from that distant night when my mother presented my father with a plate adorned with eggs, sausage, and… unmistakably burnt biscuits.

Anxious anticipation gripped me as I awaited my father's reaction. Yet, to my surprise, his response was not one of dismay but of warmth. With a gentle smile, he reached for the charred biscuit, casting a glance of appreciation towards my mother, and then engaged me in conversation about my day at school. While my response fades in the memory, I vividly recall him meticulously spreading butter and jelly on that charred offering, savoring every bite.

Later, as I rose from the table, I overheard my mom's hushed apology for the burnt biscuits. His response, etched forever in my mind, embodied true love: "Honey, I love burnt biscuits."

Intrigued, I crept into my dad's room that night, questioning if he truly enjoyed the offering. He chuckled, pulling me into a hug, and offered a gentle lesson: "Your Momma had a tough day, and she's tired. Besides, a little burnt biscuit never hurt anyone!"

Adapted from various versions on the internet.

Ponder this:

The story of the burnt biscuit extends far beyond a cooking mistake. It shows us something deeper about love and family. When we forgive small mistakes and focus on love and understanding instead of criticism, we build stronger bonds with our loved ones. Prioritizing compassion creates a warm and caring atmosphere for everyone.

The Tale of the Sands

A stream, born in distant mountains, traveled across varied landscapes until it reached the sands of the desert. It had overcome every obstacle thus far, so it believed it could conquer this one, too. Yet, as the stream poured into the desert, its waters vanished into the sands. The stream felt certain its destiny was to cross the desert and reach the sea, but no matter what it tried, it seemed there was no way forward.

Before long, the stream heard a voice whispering from the desert itself, “The wind crosses the desert, so can you.”

“Yes, but the wind can fly!” the stream cried, still throwing itself into the sands.

“You’ll never get across that way,” the desert whispered once again. “You’ll have to let the wind carry you.”

“But how?” cried out the stream.

“You have to let the wind absorb you.”

The stream balked at the idea. It had never been absorbed before; it didn’t want to lose its identity. “If I give myself to the wind, how can I know I will ever be a stream again?”

“The wind,” replied the desert, “carries water over the desert and then releases it as rain. Falling again, the water becomes a river once more.”

The desert warned that the stream could choose to continue flowing into the sands, but that would eventually lead to it becoming a swamp or a stagnant puddle. It could never cross the desert by remaining as it was.

The stream protested: “Why can’t I remain as I am?”

"You cannot stay the same," replied the desert. "Either you give yourself to the wind or become a swamp. By surrendering to the wind, your essential part will be carried away and reborn as a stream on the other side."

The stream could not believe it but realized that the best that could be attained without attempting the suggestion would be to become a swamp. Either way, the stream could not stay as it was.

The stream hesitated. Silently, it listened to its inner voice, remembering ancient memories of once being held by the wind. Finally, the stream surrendered to the sun's heat, allowing its vapors to rise into the welcoming embrace of the wind. It was carried in great white clouds over the desert. The water returned as gentle rain on the far side, trickling down rocky slopes. Gradually, it gained strength, flowing as a swift stream toward the sea.

~ Adapted from *Tales of the Dervishes* (Idries Shah)

Ponder this:

This moving tale of a stream traversing a vast desert offers a profound reflection on the nature of change. The desert's wisdom serves as a powerful metaphor. Just as the wind transforms water into vapor, allowing it to traverse the desert and be reborn as a stream, so too must we embrace transformation if we are to reach our full potential. Clinging rigidly to who we are or how we've always done things can leave us stagnant, like a puddle evaporating in the desert sun.

The story reminds us that change is inevitable. Life throws challenges and new situations our way, demanding adaptation. The key lies not in resisting this change, but in embracing its transformative potential. By surrendering to the "wind" of new experiences and opportunities, we allow ourselves to be carried to new heights, eventually reforming into a stronger, more evolved version of ourselves. Just as the stream, initially apprehensive, ultimately found its way to the sea through transformation, so too can we navigate life's obstacles by embracing the winds of change.

A Tale of Two Shoe Salesmen

Two enterprising shoe salesmen embarked on a trip to a developing nation, seeking to expand their business horizons. Upon arrival, one salesman was overwhelmed by the sight of a population largely without shoes. Dejected, he contacted his wife, lamenting, "There's no point in staying here. No one wears shoes, so there are no customers!" He promptly booked the next flight home, defeated by the perceived lack of opportunity.

The other salesman, however, saw a world of possibility in the same situation. Excitedly, he called his wife and exclaimed, " Honey, you won't believe it! This is a goldmine! Nobody here has shoes – the entire country is a potential customer base!"

Adapted from various versions on the internet.

Ponder this:

Opportunity is often disguised by challenge. Our perspective shapes our reality. The first salesman perceived the lack of shoes as an insurmountable obstacle, while the second saw it as an untapped market teeming with potential.

This tale highlights the power of a positive mindset. When we approach challenges with optimism and a willingness to see the potential within difficulties, we open ourselves up to a world of possibilities and pave the way for success.

Edmund Hillary: Conquering Mount Everest

New Zealand's Edmund Hillary and Nepalese sherpa, Tenzing Norgay became legends on May 29, 1953, when they etched their names in history as the first climbers to summit Mount Everest, the Earth's highest peak at a staggering 8,848 meters (29,032 feet). This singular achievement catapulted Hillary to international fame and a knighthood – he was Sir Edmund Hillary practically overnight. However, his ascent to the peak mirrored his personal growth – a challenging journey that demanded resilience and unwavering determination.

The summit of Everest had claimed numerous expeditions since 1922. Failure was a familiar story before Hillary's triumphant ascent in 1953. He himself had participated in two previous attempts. In 1951, a British reconnaissance expedition to Everest fell short of its goal. The following year, Hillary joined another expedition targeting Cho Oyu, a Himalayan peak west of Everest, but this attempt too was thwarted due to the lack of a viable route on the Nepalese side.

Despite these setbacks, Hillary was invited to speak in England. As he walked on stage to thunderous applause, a peculiar dissonance arose within him. The audience hailed him as a champion for attempting greatness, yet Hillary felt undeserving. He hadn't achieved his ultimate goal – Everest remained unconquered.

In a defining moment during his speech, Hillary strayed from the microphone, his gaze fixated on a picture of Everest adorning the wall. In a defiant gesture, he pointed his clenched fist at the picture and declared, "Mount Everest, you beat me the first time, but I'll beat you the next time because you've grown all you are going to grow, and I'm still growing." This powerful statement embodied his unwavering spirit.

Adapted from various versions on the internet.

Ponder this:

Edmund Hillary's encounter with Mount Everest went beyond a physical challenge; it was a journey of personal growth. His resolute declaration before the picture of Everest wasn't just bravado, but a testament to his unflinching resolve. Just a year later, he would stand atop the world, not only conquering Everest but also his own self-doubt.

Just as Hillary refused to be defined by his failures, we too can harness the lessons learned from our struggles to propel ourselves towards our goals. By adopting a growth mindset and unwavering determination, we can conquer our own personal Everests.

Bruce Lee - Wisdom of Yoda

Sweat dripped from Master Chong's brow as he bowed before Bruce Lee. "Esteemed Master Lee," he pleaded, his voice heavy with reverence, "your prowess is unmatched! I beseech you, impart upon me your wisdom, all that you know of martial arts!"

Bruce, ever the stoic teacher, regarded Master Chong with a calm gaze. In his hands, he held two identical teacups, each filled to the brim with steaming liquid. He held them out to Master Chong.

"Master Chong," Bruce began, his voice a quiet rasp, "imagine that the first cup represents all the knowledge you've accumulated throughout your martial arts journey. Years of relentless training, countless techniques – it all resides within this cup."

Master Chong's eyes flicked from Bruce's face to the brimming cup, a flicker of recognition crossing his features. He nodded eagerly.

Bruce continued, his other hand lifting the second cup. "This cup, my friend, represents the entirety of my own martial arts knowledge. Techniques honed to perfection; philosophies passed down through generations."

He gestured between the two cups. "Now, Master Chong, you ask me to fill you with my knowledge. But tell me, where would I pour it if your cup is already full?"

A frown creased Master Chong's brow. He clenched and unclenched his fists, the weight of Bruce's words settling in. Could it be that his years of training, his cherished techniques, were somehow… hindering him?

A wry smile touched Bruce's lips. "Before I can teach you, Master Chong, you must first empty your cup. Let go of what you think you know. Only then can you begin to truly learn."

(Lee, 2007)

Ponder this:

Bruce Lee's advice reminds us of something Yoda, the wise Jedi Master, would say: "Unlearn what you have learned." This statement, despite its seeming absurdity, holds immense power. Real progress frequently requires letting go of outdated beliefs and practices. When we clear out our minds, we create space for new knowledge and refined skills to take root. This helps us move forward with a clearer vision and stronger determination.

The Ben Hogan Comeback

Legendary golfer Ben Hogan embodies the unwavering spirit of a true champion. This story exemplifies his relentless pursuit of excellence, even in the face of adversity.

In the early 1950s, during a Texas tournament plagued by brutal weather – frigid temperatures, pouring rain, and strong winds – Hogan defied expectations. He delivered a masterful performance, outperforming the competition by a staggering five strokes. Yet, even after this remarkable victory, his focus remained unwavering.

A curious young reporter, eager to understand Hogan's legendary work ethic, approached him after the round. As Hogan resumed practicing despite the harsh conditions, the reporter inquired, "Mr. Hogan, you've just played a spectacular round in appalling weather. Why are you back out here practicing in the rain?"

Without breaking focus, Hogan continued hitting balls towards his distant caddy, his voice gruff as he replied, "I practice because I hope to play just as well again tomorrow."

This anecdote highlights Hogan's relentless dedication to his craft. It wasn't simply about winning one tournament; it was about constant improvement and maintaining peak performance.

Hogan's dedication extends far beyond rain-soaked practice sessions. In 1949, a horrific car accident nearly claimed his life. Before the actual collision, Hogan saved his wife, Valerie from serious injury by throwing himself over her at the last second, but his own legs were crushed. Blood clots rising from his injured legs toward his lungs and brain threatened his life.

At the hospital, the doctors told his wife, "Mrs. Hogan, your husband will not survive the night." His wife quietly said, "You obviously don't know my husband."

Hogan defied the odds. He underwent a risky surgery, pulled through, and began a grueling rehabilitation. Doctors told Valerie, "Ben will never walk again." Once more, her resolute response echoed: "You obviously don't know my husband."

As the months went by, Ben began to get his spirit back again. Although he realized that he was in a hospital bed with his body badly damaged, he decided that he was going to play golf again. The doctors were astounded when they learnt of his intent and they said to his wife, "Mrs. Hogan, Ben now wants his golf clubs strung up on the ceiling where he can see them all day long, but he is never going to play golf again." Valerie, however, knew her husband's character better, and she famously responded, "You obviously don't know my husband."

Hogan's spirit proved unbreakable. He endured grueling physical therapy and, with incredible determination, returned to the golf course within ten months. Despite the pain and physical limitations, he resumed winning major tournaments.

From 1950 to 1953, Hogan scaled even greater golfing heights than before the accident. He captured the bulk of his nine major titles, including three victories in a single year (1953): the U.S. Open, British Open, and Masters. He remained a dominant force well into the 1960s.

Adapted from various versions on the internet.

Ponder this:

Ben Hogan's story goes beyond the realm of sports. It's proof of the power of a champion's mindset, which consists of unshakeable belief that everything is possible, unyielding drive, and a tireless pursuit of excellence. It reminds us that even in the face of immense challenges, the human spirit can overcome seemingly insurmountable odds.

God Answers a Call for Help

A devout man, caught in a raging flood, clung to his faith. He'd always found solace in prayer, and unwavering trust in God's providence. Now, in peril, he pleaded for rescue.

A large log drifted by, offering a lifeline. Yet, convinced of a grander divine plan, he let it pass. Hope flickered again as a small boat approached. Fear of seasickness, however, made him decline the help.

Desperation mounted as his strength waned. He cried out to the heavens, and a helicopter materialized. A rescue ladder descended, but the man, fixated on a direct act of God, refused.

Tragically, he succumbed to the floodwaters, his faith seemingly unanswered.

Upon reaching the afterlife, he confronted God, his voice laced with betrayal. "Where were you? Why didn't you save me?"

God replied gently, "My help arrived in many forms: the log, the boat, the helicopter. But you turned away from each. What more did you expect?"

The story serves as a reminder that divine intervention can manifest in unexpected ways. Sometimes, faith requires not just prayer, but the discernment to recognize and accept the help that comes our way.

Adapted from various versions on the internet.

Ponder this:

This story goes beyond simply questioning why good people sometimes experience awful things. It dives deep into faith and how we trust the journey we're on. It encourages us to be thoughtful about what we believe while keeping our faith strong. When we stay open to the idea that blessings can come in unexpected ways, we're more likely to notice and appreciate the support that comes our way. This can make our spiritual journey more meaningful and help us feel closer to something greater than ourselves.

The Emperor and the Seed

An emperor in the Far East was growing old and knew it was time to choose his successor. Instead of choosing one of his assistants or his children, he decided something different. He called young people in the kingdom together one day. He said, "It is time for me to step down and choose the next emperor. I have decided to choose one of you."

The kids were shocked! But the emperor continued. "I am going to give each one of you a seed today. One very special seed. I want you to plant the seed, water it and come back here one year from today with what you have grown from this one seed. I will then judge the plants that you bring, and the one I choose will be the next emperor!"

One boy named Ling was there that day and he, like the others, received a seed. He went home and excitedly told his mother the story. She helped him get a pot and planting soil, and he planted the seed and watered it carefully. Every day he would water it and watch to see if it had grown. After about three weeks, some of the other youths began to talk about their seeds and the plants that were beginning to grow.

Ling kept checking his seed, but nothing ever grew. Three weeks, 4 weeks, 5 weeks went by. Still nothing. By now, others were talking about their plants but Ling didn't have a plant, and he felt like a failure. Six months went by-still nothing in Ling's pot. He just knew he had killed his seed.

Everyone else had trees and tall plants, but he had nothing. Ling didn't say anything to his friends, however. He just kept waiting for his seed to grow.

A year finally went by and all the youths of the kingdom brought their plants to the emperor for inspection. Ling told his mother that he wasn't going to take an empty pot, but his mother insisted that he be honest about what had happened. Ling felt sick to his stomach, but he knew his mother was right. He took his empty pot to the palace. When Ling arrived, he was amazed at the variety of plants grown by the other youths. They were beautiful-in all shapes and sizes. Ling put his empty pot on the floor and many of the other kinds laughed at him. A few felt sorry for him and just said, "Hey nice try."

When the emperor arrived, he surveyed the room and greeted the young people. Ling just tried to hide in the back. "My, what great plants, trees and flowers you have grown," said the emperor. "Today, one of you will be appointed the next emperor!" All of a sudden, the emperor spotted Ling at the back of the room with his empty pot. He ordered his guards to bring him to the front. Ling was terrified. "The emperor knows I'm a failure! Maybe he will have me killed!"

When Ling got to the front, the emperor asked his name. "My name is Ling," he replied. All the kids were laughing and making fun of him. The emperor asked everyone to quiet down. He looked at Ling, and then announced to the crowd, "Behold your new emperor! His name is Ling!" Ling couldn't believe it. Ling couldn't even grow his seed. How could he be the new emperor?

Then the emperor said, "One year ago today, I gave everyone here a seed. I told you to take the seed, plant it, water it, and bring it back to me today. But I gave you all boiled seeds which would not grow. All of you, except Ling, have brought me trees and plants and flowers. When you found that the seed would not grow, you substituted another seed for the one I gave you. Ling was the only one with the courage and honesty to bring me a pot with my seed in it. Therefore, he is the one who will be the new emperor!"

(The Emperor and The Seed, 2011)

Ponder this:

The emperor's seemingly harsh test is like a big life lesson. It's not about how much we achieve on the outside, but about staying true to who we are on the inside. This story shows us that real leadership comes from being honest and doing the right thing.

Just like Ling grew into a better person by being truthful, we can also shine by being genuine and doing what's right. The story reminds us not to cheat or lie to get ahead. It's when we stick to honesty that we can become our best selves and inspire others to do the same.

The Curious Wanderer's Dilemma

A man lived near a mountain. Almost every day he contemplated: What would it feel like to reach the summit of that mountain? And, once at the top, what would I see?

At last, his insatiable curiosity overcame him, and he resolved to attempt the climb.

He packed a few necessities and set out on his quest.

He encountered the first traveller as he arrived at the base of the mountain.

"What did you see from the top of the mountain and how did you get there?", he inquired.

Thus, the traveller conveyed both his route and his perspective.

However, the man thought to himself, "It sounds like a pretty exhausting way to go."

I must find another route.

So, he kept strolling along the mountain's base till he encountered the next traveller.

And, he enquired once more: "How did you ascend that mountain and what did you view from the summit?"

The traveller narrated his experience.

The man remained undecided about which route he should take, so he asked another thirty people who had completed the climb to the summit.

Upon concluding his conversations with each of them individually, he finally made up his mind: "I don't need to climb there anymore since so many individuals have already shared with me their routes and especially what they all saw from the summit."

It is indeed unfortunate that this man chose not to make the climb.

Adapted from various versions on the internet.

Ponder this:

By always asking for advice and listening only to others, the man in the story misses out on something important: everyone's journey is different. True understanding and happiness come from experiencing things for yourself. He also forgets how valuable the journey itself is, getting too caught up in reaching the end and what others say about it.

The story shows us how thinking too much, being unsure, and being scared of failing can stop us from growing, trying new things, and finding out who we really are. It tells us to take chances, face challenges, and chase our dreams with courage and determination, even when things seem tough or uncertain.

The Patient Elephant

An elephant and a dog became pregnant at the same time. Three months later, the dog welcomed a litter of six playful pups. Six months further on, she was pregnant again, and soon presented another litter of healthy puppies. This pattern continued over time.

Eighteen months in, the dog, surrounded by her growing pack, approached the elephant and asked, "Are you sure you're pregnant? We became pregnant at the same time, and I've already given birth to over a dozen puppies! They're all big dogs now, yet you're still carrying yours. What's going on?"

The elephant, wise and patient, responded, "Dear friend, what I carry is no ordinary pup; it's an elephant. I give birth only once every two years. When my baby enters the world, the earth itself trembles. When it crosses the path, humans stand in awe. My burden is monumental."

Adapted from various versions on the internet.

Ponder this:

Don't despair if others seem to receive blessings sooner than you. Don't envy their journeys. Comparing your journey to another's only hinders your own growth. Every path unfolds in its own time. Flowers bloom at different times, usually when they will have the best chance to survive and thrive. In like manner, trust your own path and embrace the unique unfolding of your story. When your time arrives, your moment will come, and it too will be worthy of admiration.

The Three Laughing Monks

Once upon a time in ancient China, there were three old monks who travelled together. Their names remain lost to history, as they never disclosed them to anyone. People called them the "Three Laughing Monks" because all they did was laugh.

Whenever they reached a village or town, they stood in the main square and started laughing. Their infectious joyfulness gradually enveloped everyone around them, creating an ever-growing laughing crowd. Eventually, the entire village or town joined in the laughter. Then, the monks moved on to the next village, spreading joy wherever they went.

These monks didn't speak to anyone; their laughter was their only form of prayer and teaching. People all over China loved and respected them because they showed that life should be enjoyed and laughed at. They travelled around China, making people laugh and feel happy for many years.

One day, while they were in a village in the northern province, one of the monks died. The villagers gathered, expecting sorrow and tears from the remaining two. But to their astonishment, the surviving monks laughed even harder.

"Why no mourning?" the villagers asked.

As they had never spoken to anyone else before, their response came unexpectedly: "Yesterday, on our way to your village, our departed friend made a bet on which of us would be the first to pass away. And now he has won. The old rogue even left a last will and testament. In it, he asked to be cremated in his old clothes because he had always stayed clean through his laughter."

As the monks lit the funeral pyre, fireworks of many colors exploded, surprising everyone. The villagers joined in the laughter of the two wise monks, realizing that their friend had left them with one final act of mischief… Chinese fireworks!

Adapted from various versions on the internet.

Ponder this:

The story of the Three Laughing Monks isn't just funny; it's a lesson about life. It shows us that life isn't all about being sad or serious. Laughter is like a refreshing rain that washes away our worries and sadness. It's a reminder that happiness is right here, in the moment we're in.

Let's take a cue from these wise monks and approach each moment with a light heart. Let laughter be our compass as we journey through life.

The Parable of Brother Leo

A legend tells of a French monastery known throughout Europe for the extraordinary leadership of a man known only as Brother Leo. Several monks began a pilgrimage to visit Brother Leo to learn from him. Almost immediately, they began to bicker about who should do various chores.

On the third day they met another monk going to the monastery, and he joined them. This monk never complained or shirked a duty, and whenever the others would fight over a chore, he would gracefully volunteer and do it himself. By the last day, the others were following his example, and from then on they worked together harmoniously.

When they reached the monastery and asked to see Brother Leo, the man who greeted them laughed.

'But our brother is among you!' And he pointed to the fellow who had joined them late in the trip.

Adapted from various versions on the internet.

Ponder this:

The story shows us a special kind of leadership called servant leadership. It's when leaders focus on helping others instead of just being in charge, on giving rather than taking, and on doing things instead of ordering them. In this style, leaders lead by showing, not just telling. Real leadership isn't about giving orders; it's about inspiring and motivating by what you do.

Brother Leo is a great example of this. He quietly showed the value of working together and putting others first. His actions turned a group of arguing pilgrims into a united team, proving how leading by example can make a big difference. By learning from humble leaders like Brother Leo, we can all become better leaders, no matter what role we're in.

A Lesson in Goal Achievement

The story of Japan's post-war economic rise offers a compelling lesson in the power of ambitious goal setting and unwavering commitment.

Devastation and Determination: In 1950, a war-torn Japan, devoid of natural resources, embarked on a seemingly audacious mission: becoming the world leader in textile manufacturing. Their unwavering commitment, fueled by a collective national spirit, propelled them to achieve this goal within a decade.

Repeating the Formula: Buoyed by their initial success, Japan set a new target in the 1960s – becoming the top steel producer. This goal appeared even more absurd, as Japan lacked domestic iron ore. Yet, their determination was undeterred. They devised innovative strategies, importing iron ore and building efficient steel mills, ultimately achieving their goal by the decade's end.

A Near Miss and Continued Success: The 1970s saw them set their sights on automobile manufacturing dominance. Although they narrowly missed their target year, achieving it a year later demonstrated their relentless pursuit of excellence.

The Electronics Era: The 1980s witnessed Japan's focus shift towards electronics and computers. Their dedication to this goal is evident in the ubiquity of Japanese-made electronics, particularly televisions, in the American market.

Adapted from various versions on the internet.

Ponder this:

This story transcends national borders. It emphasizes the importance of setting ambitious goals that push us beyond what we think we can do. It also teaches us about the strength of working together and the determination it takes to conquer challenges and achieve amazing results. When we adopt these ideas, whether as individuals, families, teams, or entire nations, we can use goal setting to accomplish incredible things.

The Pipeline Story

There was once a small mountain village where the natives were dependent upon a spring in the center of their village. One day the spring suddenly ran dry. There was another spring and reservoir a few miles away but it was too far for the villagers to travel.

The village leaders called an emergency meeting to discuss the issue. Two villagers offered to take on the task of delivering water to the village on a daily basis. The elders awarded independent contracts to each of them. They felt that a little competition would keep prices low and ensure a backup supply of water.

The first of the two people, Ed, immediately ran out, bought two galvanized steel buckets and began running back and forth along the trail to the reservoir.

He immediately began making money as he labored morning till dusk hauling water from the reservoir with his two buckets. He would empty them into the large concrete holding tank the villagers had built.

Each morning he arose much earlier than the rest of the villagers to make sure there was enough water to meet their morning needs. It was hard work, but he was very happy to be making money and for having one of the two exclusive contracts for this business.

The second winning contractor, Bill, disappeared for a while. He was not seen for months, which made Ed very happy since he had no competition. Ed was making all the money.

Instead of buying two buckets to compete with Ed, Bill had created a plan, found four investors, and returned six months later with a construction crew. Within a year his team had built a large volume stainless steel pipeline, which connected the village holding tank to the reservoir.

At the grand opening celebration, Bill announced that his water was cleaner than Ed's water. Bill knew that there had been complaints about dirt in Ed's water.

Bill also announced that he could supply the village with water 24 hours a day, seven days a week. Ed could only deliver water on the weekdays. He did not work on weekends.

Then Bill announced that he would charge 75% less than Ed did for this higher quality and more reliable supply. The village cheered and ran immediately for the faucet at the end of Bill's pipeline.

In order to compete, Ed also lowered his rates by 75%, bought two more buckets, added covers to his buckets, and began hauling four buckets each trip. In order to improve his service, he employed his two sons to give him a hand for the night shift and on weekends.

Bill, the pipeline builder, however, began enjoying the fruits of his labor. He drastically reduced his work hours and began enjoying the income his venture generated. He found the pipeline required minimal maintenance, so he was free to spend his days fishing the mountain streams and enjoying time with his kids.

Many years later, after both men had died, the pipeline was still an integral part of village life and the pipeline builder's children continued to enjoy the benefits of their father's entrepreneurial spirit.

(Kiyosaki, 2000)

Ponder this:

This story teaches an important lesson for anyone chasing a goal. Here's what we can take away from it:

- Look ahead: Think about solutions that will benefit you in the long run, not just right now.

- Build systems: Creating efficient systems can save you time and effort by automating tasks.
- Plan for tomorrow: Consider how your choices today will shape your future and affect those around you.

By being strategic and focusing on long-term gains rather than short-term rewards, we can achieve greater success and build a more sustainable future.

The Monkey Trap

In regions with abundant monkeys, locals have developed a cunning method for capture. The simplicity is deceptive. They use a gourd (think coconut) or similar object, cutting a hole just big enough for a monkey's hand to pass through. To weigh it down, they add sand or pebbles. Inside, they place a tempting nut or fruit, then leave it where monkeys can find it.

The scenario unfolds predictably. The monkey reaches in, grabs the treat, but the clenched fist is too large to escape the hole. The gourd, now heavy with the prize, is cumbersome for the creature to carry.

Here's the crux: because the monkey refuses to let go of the food, it becomes trapped. Freedom is surrendered for a meager morsel.

Escape requires nothing more than releasing the bait. Yet, the monkey views the treat as its possession and clings to it, remaining imprisoned.

The true trap lies not in the gourd, but within the monkey's mind. It's the attachment to the possession and the unwillingness to let go.

Adapted from various versions on the internet.

Ponder this:

The story paints a powerful picture about the pitfalls of attachment. It highlights a crucial human failing: our tendency to cling to things, even when they're not good for us. Like the monkey, we often become prisoners of our attachments, sacrificing freedom and happiness for the sake of holding on.

But not all attachments are bad. To reach our full potential, we need to let go of things that hold us back, like harboring negativity, clinging to material possessions, or holding on to the past. By letting go, we can feel lighter and expose ourselves to greater opportunities.

Looking Up

Back in the days of sailing ships, a young sailor went to sea for the first time. The ship encountered a heavy storm in the North Atlantic. The young sailor was commanded to go aloft and trim the sails. As the young sailor started to climb, he made the mistake of looking down. The roll of the ship combined with the tossing of the waves, made for a frightening experience. The young man started to lose his balance. At that moment, an older sailor underneath him shouted, "Look up, son, look up!" The young sailor looked up and regained his balance.

(Ziglar, 1975)

Ponder this:

This story teaches us a valuable lesson about dealing with tough times. Instead of getting bogged down by problems, it's important to change how we see things. When we focus too much on the difficulties, it can feel like everything is crashing down on us. However, by choosing to "look up" – to shift our perspective and identify potential solutions – we regain a sense of control and the courage to navigate the storm. This simple act of shifting perspective empowers us to confront challenges with courage and perseverance.

Don't Sell Yourself Short

The human race is a story of people selling themselves short and settling for less than they are capable of achieving. Instead of achievement, we get addicted to activity. In time we confuse activity with achievement.

The following story is a good analogy of how many of us live our lives.

The renowned French Naturalist, Jean-Henri Fabre, conducted an interesting experiment with processionary caterpillars, so-called because of their habit of following a lead caterpillar, each with its eyes half closed and head fitted snugly against the rear end of the preceding caterpillar.

Fabre was able to get them on to the rim of a large flowerpot with the lead caterpillar connected up to the last one, thus forming a complete circle, which started moving around in a procession, with neither beginning nor end. In the middle of the circle created by their procession, he placed some pine needles, their favorite food. Each caterpillar followed the one ahead thinking that it was heading for the food.

The naturalist expected that after a while they would discover their predicament or get tired of their useless procession, and move off in some new direction. But that was not the case. Through sheer force of habit, the creeping circle of caterpillars kept moving around the rim of the pot, quite oblivious to the world around them. They were busy being busy, blindly following the caterpillar in front.

Round and round they went for seven days and nights! After a week of this mindless activity, the caterpillars started to drop dead because of exhaustion and starvation. They died with the food they were searching for just inches away. Because of their nature and this circular arrangement, they all assumed that the caterpillar in front was leading.

The processionary caterpillars were locked into this lifestyle of rigidly following their instincts, habits, past experience, tradition, custom and precedent – the way they always had done things. In reality, they got nowhere.

Adapted from various versions on the internet.

Ponder this:

This story about the processionary caterpillars teaches us a valuable lesson about falling into unproductive routines. The caterpillars confused activity with accomplishment. They confused being busy with results. Many of us are guilty of the same mistake.

Just like those caterpillars, we often become engrossed in a relentless cycle of "doing" - we confuse staying busy with making real progress. But unlike them, we have the ability to think and make choices. This story encourages us to break free from repetitive cycles, to pause and think about whether what we're doing is truly helping us reach our goals.

The $25,000 Idea

Sometime in the early 1900s there was an efficiency consultant named Ivy Lee, who had a meeting with the president of a small US steel company. During this meeting the president explained to him that he felt that his company had the knowledge and skills it needed to move forward, but he thought they were lacking when it came to "getting things done". The reason he had requested to meet with Mr. Lee was because he hoped that he could provide him with a solution to this problem.

After listening to the president's thoughts, Ivy Lee said that in less than 15 minutes he could show him how to accomplish his goal if he agreed to try the solution for at least a couple of weeks and then to pay him what he thought the idea was worth. The president happily agreed and Ivy Lee gave the following advice:

Each day, at the end of the day, take out a sheet of paper. Write down the six most important things you have to do the next day. Then rank those items in the order of importance. When you come in the next morning, take out the paper and start with item 1. When you have finished that item, move on to number 2 (and so on down the list). If you cannot complete an item because of external factors, skip it and move on to the next one. At the end of the day make another list of the six most important items you have to do the next day....

After the meeting, which hadn't lasted more than 30 minutes, the president started using this system on a daily basis. After a short period of time, he saw a dramatic increase in the efficiency at which he was able to get things done, so he passed this idea along to his department managers and asked them to pass it on to others within the company.

A few weeks later, Ivy Lee received a letter from the steel company president thanking him for his advice that included a check for $25,000. Thus, this simple idea has become known as "The $25,000 Idea".

It is said that years later the company president commented that this was the best investment he had ever made, and that this single idea had a serious contribution to the company's growth from a small firm to an industry leader.

Adapted from various versions on the internet.

Ponder this:

"The $25,000 Idea" must have had an immediate and impressive impact on the steel company because, in today's value, that $25,000 would be worth more than $500,000… and now the idea is yours, *absolutely free!*

By prioritizing tasks, we can increase our productivity and achieve our goals more efficiently. This simple technique can be applied to any aspect of our lives, whether it's work, school, or personal projects.

The 7 Wonders of the World

A group of school children were asked to list what they thought were the present "Seven Wonders of the World." Though there were some disagreements, the following received the most votes:

- Egypt's Great Pyramids
- Taj Mahal
- Grand Canyon
- Panama Canal
- Empire State Building
- St. Peter's Basilica
- Great Wall of China

While gathering the votes, the teacher noted that one student had not finished her list yet. So, she asked the girl if she was having trouble with her list.

The little girl replied, "Yes, a little. I couldn't quite make up my mind because there are so many."

The teacher said, "Well, tell us what you have, and maybe we can help." The girl hesitated, then read, "I think the 'Seven Wonders of the World' are:

To see. To hear. To smell. To taste. To feel. To laugh. To love."

The room was so quiet you could hear a pin drop. The things we overlook as simple and ordinary and that we take for granted are truly wondrous.

Adapted from various versions on the internet.

Ponder this:

The little girl's list of the seven wonders of the world is a testament to the fact that we should treasure and value the things we take for granted, such as our senses, emotions, and relationships.

The Roger Bannister Story

For decades, the four-minute mile was considered an insurmountable barrier in athletics. Scientists believed the human body simply couldn't withstand the physical demands of running a mile at such a blistering pace. Then came Roger Bannister. In 1954, he defied these limitations, shattering the record and clocking in at an astonishing 3:59.4.

This feat proved to be a watershed moment. Within a year, 37 other runners broke the four-minute barrier, followed by another 300 within three years. Today, thousands have surpassed this once-unthinkable feat, constantly pushing the boundaries of human potential.

The mile run is no longer an Olympic or World Championship event, but its legacy endures. The current world record of 3:43.13, set by Hicham El Guerrouj in 1999, stands as a testament to the transformative power of breaking down perceived limitations.

Adapted from various versions on the internet.

Ponder this:

The Roger Bannister story is a great example of how beliefs can hold us back until someone breaks through them. When Bannister broke the record, it motivated many others to push their limits and achieve new heights. This story shows us that when we challenge what we think is possible, we open up a world of opportunities and inspire others to do the same.

Jim Carrey and the $10 Million Check

Jim Carrey's journey to Hollywood stardom is a testament to the power of focused ambition. Long before his name became synonymous with comedic brilliance, Carrey harbored a burning desire for wealth and fame. According to Biography Channel, he manifested this dream in a unique way: by writing himself a post-dated check for $10 million, payable on Thanksgiving 1995. The memo line simply read, "For Acting Services Rendered." At the time, Carrey's bank account barely boasted ten thousand dollars, a stark contrast to the astronomical sum he envisioned.

Undeterred by this financial gap, Carrey possessed unwavering faith in his aspirations. The road to success, however, was paved with challenges. He encountered obstacles that might have discouraged lesser spirits, but Carrey persevered. His relentless drive propelled him forward, and his gamble on his own potential paid off in spectacular fashion.

Carrey's career skyrocketed, surpassing the $10 million mark many times over. He commanded a staggering $20 million salary for "The Cable Guy" in 1996, followed by another $20 million for "Liar Liar" in 1997. By 2003, his fee for "Bruce Almighty" had climbed to a phenomenal $25 million. Reports suggest his average earnings per film has since exceeded $20 million! (wiki.answers.com)

Adapted from various versions on the internet.

Ponder this:

Jim Carrey's story isn't a stroke of luck; it's a testament to the power of focused intention. Many high achievers share similar experiences, demonstrating the profound impact of believing in oneself and setting audacious goals. Carrey's journey serves as an inspiration, urging us to embrace our dreams and actively pursue them with dogged determination.

The Maserati

A businessman dreamt of owning a Maserati as a reward for achieving a specific income goal. He cut out a full-page picture of his desired car from a "Wheels" magazine and proudly displayed it on his wall.

He drove a worn-out old car at the time, but his imagination transformed him into a Maserati owner whenever he was behind the wheel. He'd carefully back out of the garage, imagining his neighbors watching as he cruised off with the windows down, reveling in the luxury of leather seats, a wood-grain dashboard, and a premium sound system. Even at traffic lights, he envisioned other drivers admiring his imaginary Maserati.

Years later, he finally reached his financial target and walked into a dealership, excited to choose the exact color of his dream car.

A few weeks later, the dealership contacted him for a special "presentation" to receive it. However, upon arrival, he encountered a problem: "This isn't the exact color I ordered," he pointed out, noting the slight shade difference.

The dealership acknowledged the error and offered a significant discount, but the customer remained dissatisfied. He refused their offer, expressing disappointment over the color. The officials huddled together and returned with another proposal: they had a Maserati in his desired color, but it was a more expensive sports edition and formerly a show car featuring thousands of dollars in extras. Despite being a more expensive edition, they offered it at no extra cost.

Hesitant, he replied, "I didn't wait all this time for a used car." The officials insisted, "It's not a used car; it's practically new with minimal mileage." They encouraged him to at least see the car before making a final decision. Initially resistant, he agreed to check it only to confirm the color.

Upon entering the showroom, he was speechless. The car exceeded even his wildest dreams. Concealing his excitement from the salespeople, he meticulously inspected the vehicle for flaws, finding none. Thrilled by its upgraded features, he finally said, “Alright, I’ll take it.” Everyone involved was pleased.

After the presentation, he proudly drove his dream car home. As he entered his house, he glanced at the Maserati picture on his wall and suddenly realized that the car parked in his driveway was the exact one in the picture! It was a snapshot of his very own Maserati from a motor show – a testament to the power of visualization and steadfast determination.

Adapted from an audio program.

Ponder this:

It seemed like an amazing coincidence, but this tale goes beyond mere coincidence. It reveals little-known subtleties of the Law of Attraction, especially highlighting the power of focused vision combined with steadfast determination.

The businessman’s steadfast belief, fueled by the constant visual reminder on his wall, not only kept his dream alive but ultimately manifested it in a way that even exceeded his initial expectations. The story reminds us that visualization is most effective when coupled with persistent action towards achieving one’s goals. The businessman’s years of hard work to reach his financial target were as crucial to his success as the power of his imagination.

Clearly, the Universe conspires to help you. When you do your part, it does its part in weird and wonderful ways (like causing a dealership “error” and then being presented with a “used” car that turned out to be “the exact one” that was envisioned). Mind-boggling, to say the least!

Do Something

In the depths of despair, a man, overwhelmed by the relentless tide of pain and suffering surrounding him, collapsed to his knees and pounded the earth in frustration.

With tear-streaked cheeks turned towards the heavens, he unleashed a desperate cry to his God.

"Behold this chaos! Witness the agony and torment, the bloodshed and malice! Oh God, why do you remain silent? WHY DON'T YOU DO SOMETHING?"

And in that moment of anguish, a divine whisper pierced the darkness, reaching the depths of his soul.

"I have," spoke the voice, gentle yet resolute. "I sent you."

Ponder this:

This story really makes us think about our role in shaping the world. It's easy to blame others or outside forces for all the problems, but that just takes away our own power to make things better. Sure, we can't control everything that happens, but we can control how we react and what we do about it. Even the smallest actions can make a big difference. When we choose to be part of the solution and take responsibility for our impact, we're living up to our potential and making the world a better place.

The Three Stone Cutters

A traveller encountered three individuals engaged in stone work. Curious about their task, the traveller approached the first worker and asked, "What are you doing?" Without hesitation, the worker replied, "I am a stone cutter, shaping these stones."

Still uncertain, the traveller approached the second worker and posed the same question. The second worker paused, glanced at the traveller, and explained, "I am a stone cutter. I shape these stones to earn money and provide for my family."

Perplexed by the divergent responses, the sojourner approached the third worker and inquired, "What are you doing?" Pausing, the worker studied the stone in hand, then turned to the traveller and declared, "I am a stone mason. I am constructing a cathedral – a sanctuary that will inspire people from all corners of the world to seek solace."

Remarkable! Three men, labouring side by side, each imbued with a distinct perspective: the first as a labourer performing temporary work, the second as a skilled craftsman with a career, and the third as a visionary with a sacred mission.

Adapted from a traditional tale.

Ponder this:

It is important to have a sense of purpose and a vision for one's work. When we see our work as something greater than ourselves, we are more likely to be motivated and inspired to do our best. This is especially true when we are faced with difficult or challenging tasks. By focusing on the bigger picture and the impact that our work can have, we can find meaning and fulfillment in even the most mundane or routine tasks.

Pray With Gratitude

In his book, Secrets of the Lost Mode of Prayer, bestselling author Gregg Braden shares a wonderful story about a Native American friend, David, who took him on a quest to bring rain during a long drought in New Mexico in the 1990s. Here is that story:

The pair had walked quite a distance to a sacred place used by David's ancestors for prayer and ritual. David took off his shoes and stepped into the circle. He acknowledged the four directions and his ancestors, placed his hands in prayer position, closed his eyes and then stood motionless in silence.

After a few moments, he said he had finished and was ready to leave.

Gregg, who was waiting for something more elaborate to happen, said, I thought you were going to pray for rain.

'No,' he replied. 'I said that I would pray rain. If I had prayed for rain, it could never happen.'

When Gregg asked him why, he said 'It's because the moment you pray for something to occur, you've just acknowledged that it's not existing in that moment – and you may actually be denying the very thing you'd like to bring forward in your prayers.'

He described how the elders of his village had shared the secrets of prayer with him when he was a young boy. The key, he said, is that when we ask for something to happen, we give power to what we do not have.

'If you pray for rain, you affirm the lack of what you want and you, therefore, create more lack of what you want – in this case, rain. When you pray rain [instead of pray for rain], you affirm the existence of rain right now, right here, in this moment. You offer gratitude for what you already have or expect to have,' he explained.

'Well, if you didn't pray for rain just now when you closed your eyes, what did you do?' asked Gregg.

He said, 'When I closed my eyes, I felt the feeling of what it feels like after there's been so much rain that I can stand with my naked feet in the mud of my pueblo village. I smelled the smells of rainwater rolling off the earthen walls of our homes. And I felt what it feels like to walk through a field of corn that is chest high because of all the rain that has fallen. In that way, I plant a seed for the possibility of that rain, and then I give thanks of gratitude and appreciation.'

'You mean gratitude for the rain that you've created?' asked Gregg.

And he said, 'No, we don't create the rain. I'm giving thanks of gratitude and appreciation for the opportunity to commune with the forces of creation.'

As the story goes, it did indeed rain thereafter.

(Braden, 2006)

Ponder this:

According to Gregg Braden, the lost mode of prayer is a prayer that's based solely in *feeling*. So, don't complain that your prayers don't work. Instead, change how you pray. Stop asking for what you want and need, and start praying to God with gratitude for *prayers answered.*

The Parable of the Butterfly

A kindhearted man discovered a butterfly cocoon and, moved by curiosity, watched the creature struggling to emerge through the tiny opening. After hours of watching the butterfly's effort, the man, driven by compassion, decided to help. He gently cut away the remaining cocoon, allowing the butterfly to escape effortlessly.

However, instead of a graceful, flying butterfly, the creature emerged with a swollen body and underdeveloped wings. The man hoped the wings would expand and lift the butterfly into the air, but his hopes were in vain. Having missed the crucial struggle, the butterfly's wings were too weak to support it in flight. Consequently, the butterfly spent its short life crawling with a swollen body and shriveled wings.

Adapted from various versions on the internet.

Ponder this:

This parable is a powerful reminder that growth often comes from overcoming challenges. Though seemingly painful, the butterfly's struggle within the cocoon served a crucial purpose. Each attempt to push through the barrier strengthened its wings, preparing it for the moment of flight.

Just as the butterfly needed its struggle to develop the strength to fly, sometimes we need to 'struggle' to break through the 'cocoons' of our lives to prepare for our evolutionary journey. Rather than seeing challenges as negative experiences, view them as opportunities for growth and evolution. Each challenge you face brings you closer to your goals, equipping you with new insights and abilities to tackle the next phase of your journey.

The Remarkable Soichiro Honda

Like most other countries, Japan was hit badly by the Great Depression of the 1930s. At this time Soichiro Honda was an expert auto mechanic with his own workshop in the city of Hahamatsu. In 1938, Soichiro Honda started a little factory to manufacture piston rings for motor car engines.

His intention was to sell the piston rings to Toyota. He labored night and day, even slept in the workshop, always believing he could perfect his design and develop a quality product. Desperate for funds, he pawned his wife's jewelry to finance his business.

Finally, the day came when he completed his piston ring and was able to take a working sample to Toyota. Toyota rejected his creation, saying that the rings did not meet their standards. Soichiro suffered ridicule when the engineers laughed at his design.

He refused to give up. Rather than focus on his failure, he continued working towards his goal. He went back to school to study metallurgy and learn how to work with metal. After two more years of struggle and a redesign of his product, he finally won a contract with Toyota in 1940.

However, at this time, the Japanese government was gearing up for war. With the contract in hand, Soichiro Honda needed to build a factory to supply Toyota, but building materials were in short supply. Still, he would not quit! He invented a new concrete-making process that enabled him to build the factory.

With the factory now built, he was ready for production, but the factory was bombed twice. Also, steel became unavailable. Was this the end of the road for Honda? No!

He started collecting surplus gasoline cans discarded by US fighters. 'Gifts from President Truman,' he called them, and they became the new raw material for his rebuilt manufacturing process. Finally, an earthquake destroyed the factory.

After the war, an extreme gasoline shortage forced people to walk or use bicycles. Riding his bicycle to work was too slow, so Soichiro built a tiny engine and attached it to his bicycle. People in his neighborhood were impressed and wanted one, too. Unfortunately, raw materials to build the engines were in short supply and he was unable to meet the demand.

Unwilling to accept defeat, Soichiro Honda wrote to 18,000 bicycle store owners and, in an inspiring letter, asked them to help him revitalize Japan. Approximately 5,000 responded and supported his quest to build his small bicycle engines. Unfortunately, the first models were too bulky to work well, so he continued to develop and adapt. Finally, the small engine named 'The Super Cub' became a reality and was an outstanding success. Having achieved success in Japan, Honda then began exporting his Super Cub motorcycles to Europe and America.

The story does not end there. In the 1970s there was another gas shortage and the automotive trend shifted to small cars. Honda was quick to pick up on the trend. Expert in small engine design, his company started making small cars, smaller than anyone had seen before, and rode another wave of success.

Today, Honda Corporation is one of the world's largest automobile companies. Honda succeeded because one man made a truly committed decision, acted upon it, and made adjustments on a continuous basis. Failure was not an option for Soichiro Honda.

Adapted from various versions on the internet.

Ponder this:

Everyone knows how to thrive in the good times. It is the trying times that separate those of true substance from those who portray an image of substance i.e. those who really walk the talk from those who merely talk.

Soichiro Honda's remarkable journey is a testament to the power of steadfast determination and resilience. Despite facing a relentless barrage of setbacks - rejection, ridicule, material shortages, war-time destruction, even natural disasters - Honda refused to be deterred. He consistently adapted his strategies, embraced continuous learning, and even transformed perceived obstacles (like discarded gasoline cans) into opportunities. His story reminds us that the path to success is rarely a straight line, and true grit lies not just in persisting through hardship, but also in learning from failures and capitalizing on unexpected possibilities.

You Are Divine

A Hindu legend beautifully illustrates the divine essence within each of us. It tells the story of a time when humans wielded divine powers, but due to misuse, Lord Brahma, the creator god, decided to hide them in a place where they would be impossible to find.

A council of lesser gods pondered suitable hiding places. One suggested burying them deep within the earth, but Lord Brahma countered that humans would eventually unearth them.

Another proposed sending their divinity to the ocean's depths, but again, he warned that exploration would eventually lead to their rediscovery.

After much thought, the lesser gods became concerned and declared, "Since human's divine powers cannot be safely concealed in either land or sea, then there is nowhere to hide them!"

Lord Brahma, with a knowing smile, proclaimed, "We shall hide them within humankind itself! For there, one never thinks to look."

Since then, the legend claims, humans have searched tirelessly for something that has always resided within them: their own divinity. This tale serves as a powerful reminder that our true potential, our divine spark, lies dormant within, waiting to be discovered and awakened.

(Baba, 2005)

Ponder this:

It is also written that people are created in the same image and likeness of God. You might be familiar with the following quote:

> *Ye are Gods and the spirit of God dwells within you.*
>
> —Corinthians 3:16

This means that you are divine. You were born this way and will always remain so. Your soul is the individualized essence of the Divine. Often, our divinity is hidden beneath layers of fear, doubt, uncertainty, sorrow, rage, unworthiness, and false assumptions from past experiences. It's our responsibility to strip away these limiting beliefs and realize that our true power lies within, hidden not in the external world, but in the depths of our own being.

Black Boots

Shelley received a gift that she desperately needed in a very unusual way. She was sitting at Notre Dame in Paris resting her sore feet. She had not brought a comfortable pair of shoes from the States, and her limited budget wouldn't allow her to buy another pair although her feet ached terribly.

Suddenly she felt prompted to walk out of the church and turn left. Following her inner promptings, she made several more turns to arrive at a square. To her surprise she saw a pair of brand-new black boots with no signs of wear in exactly her size on top of a trash can. She knew the situation was perfect and had been arranged specifically for her. If the boots had been inside the trash can, she wouldn't have pulled them out. If they had been worn before, she wouldn't have put them on. They were also so stylish that she could never have afforded them herself!

Would this be a story of intuition or synchronicity? Intuition appeared to have led her to the boots. Synchronicity provided her with precisely what she needed. The Universe virtually handed her the boots.

(Lundstrom, 1996)

Ponder this:

If it feels right, follow your intuition. You never know where it might lead. Shelley's intuition (or inner voice) guided her, leading her to the boots. Synchronicity, meanwhile, orchestrated the perfect placement of this unexpected gift.

Perhaps, when we are receptive to opportunity, even based on a hunch, the universe conspires to guide us in unexpected ways. So, trust your instincts and stay open to what's out there. Who knows, you might just stumble upon some amazing surprises along the way!

Great Value in Disaster

Thomas Edison's laboratory was virtually destroyed by fire in December, 1914. Although the damage exceeded $2 million, the buildings were only insured for $238,000 because they were made of concrete and thought to be fireproof.

Much of Edison's life's work went up in spectacular flames. Edison's 24-year-old son, Charles, frantically searched for his father and finally found him, calmly watching the scene, his face glowing in the reflection, his white hair blowing in the wind.

'My heart ached for him,' said Charles.

'He was 67 – no longer a young man – and everything was going up in flames. When he saw me, he shouted, "Charles, where's your mother?"'

When I told him I didn't know, he said, 'Find her. Bring her here. She will never see anything like this as long as she lives.'

The next morning, Edison looked at the ruins and said, 'There is great value in disaster. All our mistakes are burned up. Thank God we can start anew.'

Three weeks after the fire, Edison managed to deliver his first phonograph.

Adapted from various versions on the internet.

Ponder this:

Edison's story offers a powerful lesson about the power of attitude in the face of adversity. Even though the situation can be beyond our control, we still have complete authority over how we react.

Surveys, studies and research consistently reaffirm that 85% of success in life depends on attitude, 15% on aptitude. Changing attitudes is something we will always have to do to improve our circumstances in life.

Just like Edison, we can choose to see challenges as opportunities for growth and renewal. By cultivating a positive outlook, we empower ourselves to navigate setbacks and emerge stronger. This story reminds us that success is not simply about talent or skill (aptitude); it's also about the unwavering belief in ourselves and our ability to overcome obstacles (attitude).

We Are All Connected

An interesting experiment that illustrates our connectedness to everything else in existence was done in 1993 under the direction of the United States Army Intelligence and Security Command (INSCOM). Here are the details of that experiment.

White blood cells (leukocytes) were scraped from the mouth of a volunteer, centrifuged, and placed in a test tube. A probe from a recording polygraph (a 'lie' or emotion detector) was inserted in the tube. The donor of the cheek cells was seated in a room separate from his donated cells and shown a television program with many violent scenes. When the volunteer viewed scenes of fighting and killing, the polygraph probe detected extreme excitation in the mouth cells of the donor, despite the test tubes being in a separate room down the hallway.

Subsequent repeats of the experiment with the donor and cells separated by up to fifty miles and up to two days after they were donated showed the same results. The donated cells remained energetically, and what scientists call 'non- locally', connected with their donor and seemed to 'remember' where they came from.

(Pearsall, 1999)

Ponder this:

While the scientific validity of this particular experiment is debated, it raises interesting questions about the nature of consciousness and our connection to the world around us. The whole idea of cellular memory suggests that our cells may hold a deeper connection to us than previously understood. It forces us to consider the possibility that we are not separate beings, but rather part of a complex and interwoven energetic web.

The Power of Giving

It was a really hot summer's day many years ago. I was on my way to pick up two items at the grocery store. In those days, I was a frequent visitor to the supermarket because there never seemed to be enough money for a whole week's food-shopping at once.

You see, my young wife, after a tragic battle with cancer, had died just a few months earlier. There was no insurance, just many expenses and a mountain of bills. I held a part-time job, which barely generated enough money to feed my two young children.

Things were bad, really bad.

And so it was that day, with a heavy heart and four dollars in my pocket, I was on my way to the supermarket to purchase a gallon of milk and a loaf of bread. The children were hungry and I had to get them something to eat. As I came to a red traffic light, I noticed on my right a young man, a young woman and a child on the grass next to the road. The blistering noonday sun beat down on them without mercy.

The man held up a cardboard sign which read, 'Will Work for Food.' The woman stood next to him. She just stared at the cars that stopped at the red light. The child, probably about two years old, sat on the grass holding a one-armed doll. I noticed all this in the thirty seconds it took for the traffic light to change to green.

I wanted so desperately to give them a few dollars, but if I did that, there wouldn't be enough left to buy the milk and bread. Four dollars will only go so far. As the light changed, I took one last glance at the three of them and sped off feeling both guilty (for not helping them) and sad (because I didn't have enough money to share with them).

As I kept driving, I couldn't get the picture of the three of them out of my mind. The sad, haunting eyes of the young man and his family stayed with me for about a mile. I could take it no longer. I felt their pain and had to do something about it. I turned around and drove back to where I had last seen them.

I pulled up close to them and handed the man two of my four dollars. There were tears in his eyes as he thanked me. I smiled and drove on to the supermarket. Perhaps both milk and bread would be on sale, I thought. And what if I only got milk alone, or just the bread? Well, it would have to do.

I pulled into the parking lot, still thinking about the whole incident, yet feeling good about what I had done. As I stepped out of the car, my foot slid on something on the pavement. There by my feet was a twenty-dollar bill. I just couldn't believe it. I looked all around, picked it up with awe, went into the store and purchased not only bread and milk, but several other items I desperately needed.

I never forgot that incident. It reminded me that the universe was strange and mysterious. It confirmed my belief that you could never out give the universe. I gave away two dollars and got twenty in return. On my way back from the supermarket, I drove by the hungry family and shared five additional dollars with them.

This incident is only one of many that have occurred in my life.

It seems that the more we give, the more we get. It is, perhaps, one of those universal laws that say, 'If you want to receive, you must first give.'

~ John Harricharan (award-winning author of the bestseller, "When You Can Walk on Water, Take the Boat".)

Ponder this:

John's story moves beyond blind faith in a "Law of Giving." It highlights the power of compassion and its potential to create a chain reaction of generosity.

Some might say finding the twenty-dollar bill was 'a coincidence' or 'sheer luck'. Far from it. It was really the correct application of the Law of Giving in the particular situation. John was financially stressed at the time, yet he gave away 50% of all the money he had on him out of sheer compassion. The subtlety to the application of the law is that John selflessly gave to a needy person the very thing he needed most at that moment in his life. Think about it…

By prioritizing the needs of others, even during his own time of struggle, John set in motion a series of events that ultimately benefited both him and the family he helped. The story invites us to consider the interconnectedness of our actions and the possibility that even small acts of kindness can have unexpected and positive consequences, both for ourselves and others.

Breaking the Sound Barrier

Before Yeager's successful flight on October 14, 1947, no one had ever flown faster than the speed of sound. In fact, a previous attempt by a British pilot had ended in tragedy, underscoring the immense risks of supersonic flight.

Despite these dangers, the U.S. Air Force pushed forward with the development of the experimental Bell X-1 aircraft, explicitly designed to break the sound barrier. They needed a pilot brave enough to take on this mission, and they found that courage in Chuck Yeager. Many engineers feared the X-1 would disintegrate upon reaching supersonic speeds, but Yeager believed the intense vibrations would subside once the aircraft surpassed the sound barrier.

Fate, however, seemed determined to throw obstacles in Yeager's path. Just days before the flight, he fell off a horse and broke two ribs – an injury that could have easily disqualified him from the mission. But Yeager wasn't ready to give up. He taped up his ribs and kept quiet about his condition, determined to push forward.

On the day of the flight, another problem arose – his injured ribs made it impossible for him to shut the door of the Bell X-1. Yeager confided in Jack Ridley, the flight engineer, who ingeniously fashioned a makeshift lever from a broomstick handle so Yeager could close the hatch using his left hand.

Once in the air, Yeager faced violent vibrations that threatened to tear the aircraft apart. But he pushed on, trusting his belief that things would smooth out once the aircraft reached Mach 1. Sure enough, at Mach 0.96, the vibrations stopped, and the Bell X-1 broke through the sound barrier.

This singular feat shattered not only the sound barrier but also the prevailing doubts and limitations that had held back aviation progress. The thunderous sonic boom that echoed across the desert wasn't just the sound of breaking the sound barrier; it was the roar of human ingenuity and determination. Yeager's triumph is a powerful reminder that even the most ambitious goals can be achieved through courage, perseverance, and a willingness to face the unknown.

Ponder this:

Chuck Yeager's story isn't just about aviation – it's a lesson in tackling huge challenges. When we set ambitious goals and truly believe we can achieve them, we are ready to handle the inevitable setbacks and emerge victorious.

The story serves as a reminder that when we have bold aspirations, the universe frequently puts our resolve to the test. Yeager's bravery, tenacity, and desire to push boundaries in the face of seemingly insurmountable odds, served as the impetus for a historic accomplishment.

Circle of Joy

One day, a countryman knocked hard on a monastery door. When the monk tending the gates opened up, he was given a magnificent bunch of grapes.

"Brother, these are the finest my vineyard has produced. I've come to bear them as a gift."

"Thank you! I will take them to the Abbot immediately, he'll be delighted with this offering."

"No! I brought them for you."

"For me?" The monk blushed, for he didn't think he deserved such a fine gift of nature.

"Yes!" insisted the man. "For whenever I knock on the door, it is you who opens it. When I needed help because the crop was destroyed by drought, you gave me a piece of bread and a cup of wine every day. I hope this bunch of grapes will bring you a little of the sun's love, the rain's beauty and the miracle of God, for it is he made it grow so fine."

The monk held the grapes and spent the entire morning admiring it; it really was beautiful. Because of this, he decided to deliver the gift to the Abbot, who had always encouraged him with words of wisdom.

The Abbot was very pleased with the grapes, but he recalled that there was a sick brother in the monastery, and thought: "I'll give him the grapes. Who knows, they may bring some joy to his life."

And that is what he did. But the grapes didn't stay in the sick monk's room for long, for he reflected: "The cook has looked after me for so long, feeding me only the best meals. I'm sure he will enjoy these."

When the cook appeared at lunch, to bring him his meal, he presented him with the grapes: “They're for you,” said the sick monk. “Since you are always coming into contact with that which nature produces, you will know what to do with this work of God.”

The cook was amazed at the beauty of the grapes, and showed his assistant how perfect they were. So perfect, he thought to himself, that no one would appreciate them more than the sexton; since he was responsible for the Holy Sacrament, and many at the monastery considered him a holy man, he would be best qualified to value this marvel of nature.

The sexton, in turn, gave the grapes as a gift to the youngest novice so that he might understand that the work of God is in the smallest details of Creation. When the novice received them, his heart was filled with the Glory of the Lord, for he had never seen such beautiful grapes.

Just then, he remembered the first time he came to the monastery, and of the person who had opened the gates for him; it was that gesture which allowed him to be among this community of people who knew how to value the wonders of life.

And so, just before nightfall, he took the grapes to the monk at the gates.

“Eat and enjoy them,” he said. “For you spend most of your time alone here, and these grapes will make you very happy.”

Adapted from various versions on the internet.

Ponder this:

What goes around comes around!

True joy and fulfillment are found not in possession, but in sharing - giving without expecting anything in return. By being generous and kind, we can create a circle of joy that will continue to grow and spread, bringing happiness to ourselves and those around us.

Publisher's Appeal

If you do enjoy this book, please spread the word about it widely. It could, (as the subtitle puts it), "motivate, educate and empower" others in your sphere of influence... and beyond.

Since everything is interconnected, even a tiny act of sharing can have a big influence on other people. It may potentially create a "circle of joy" having a cascading impact that improves the lives of innumerable individuals worldwide.

Keep in mind that good deeds often pay off, and your generosity may have a long-lasting, pleasant effect on you.

Bad Temper

There once was a little boy with a terrible temper. His father, hoping to teach him a lesson, gave him a bag of nails and a hammer. The rule was simple: every time the boy lost his temper, he had to hammer a nail into the back fence.

The first day was brutal. Seething with anger, the boy hammered a staggering 37 nails into the wood. But as the days passed, the number of hammered nails dwindled. He discovered it was far easier to control his temper than expend the effort driving those nails into the fence.

Finally, a day arrived when the boy managed to control his temper entirely. Proudly, he informed his father of this feat. The father, pleased with his son's progress, suggested a new challenge: for each day the boy controlled his temper, he could pull out one nail.

Days turned into weeks, and the young boy excitedly announced to his father that all the nails were gone. The father, taking his son by the hand, led him to the fence.

"You've done well, son," the father acknowledged, "but look at the holes in the fence. The fence will never be the same. Words spoken in anger leave scars just like these. A verbal wound can be just as damaging as a physical one."

This simple story serves as a powerful reminder of the lasting impact of angry words. Just like physical wounds, the scars left by harsh words can linger, affecting relationships and leaving emotional marks.

Adapted from various versions on the internet.

Ponder this:

The story emphasizes the importance of thoughtful communication, reminding us that spoken words, once uttered, cannot be retracted. They have the power to wound and damage, just like physical blows. The emphasis is not simply on avoiding outbursts, but on choosing our words carefully, with an awareness of the potential consequences. By choosing our words carefully and expressing our emotions constructively, we can foster stronger, healthier relationships.

A Blessing in Disguise

In the northern frontier of ancient China, there lived a man who was particularly skilled in raising horses. People knew of him and called him Sai Ong – literally "Old Frontiersman."

One day, for some unknown reason, his horse got loose and ran off into the Hu territory beyond the Great Wall. The Hu tribes were hostile toward the Chinese, so everyone assumed the horse was as good as lost.

Horses were very valuable to the people living at the frontier, so they regarded this loss as a great financial setback. They visited Sai Ong to express their sympathies, but Sai Ong's elderly father surprised them by remaining calm and unaffected. Much to their puzzlement, the old man asked: "Who says this cannot be some sort of blessing?"

Months later, the horse returned to the stable with a companion – a fine steed of the Hu breed. It was as if Sai Ong's wealth suddenly doubled. Everyone came by to marvel at the new horse and to congratulate him, but again his elderly father showed no great emotions. He said: "Who says this cannot be some sort of misfortune?"

Sai Ong's son enjoyed riding and took the new horse out for a ride. An accident occurred, causing him to fall badly and break a leg. Again sympathetic people came to console the family, and again they saw that the grandfather remained as calm as ever. Just like before, he told them: "Who says this cannot be some sort of blessing?"

One year later, the Hu people amassed and crossed the border into China. All the able-bodied young men were summoned into the army to take up arms in defense. Fierce battles ensued, resulting in heavy casualties. Among the inhabitants of the northern frontier, nine out of ten men died.

Sai Ong's son did not go into battle due to his broken leg. Because of this, he was spared that terrible fate, and his family survived the war intact.

Thus, blessings may turn out to be misfortunes, and misfortunes blessings. They change from one to the other endlessly; the workings of destiny have a truly fathomless depth.

(Major, Queen, Meyer, & Roth, 2010)

Ponder this:

Every dark cloud has a silver lining or, as chapter 58 of Tao Te Ching expresses it:

Misfortune is what fortune depends upon
Fortune is where misfortune hides beneath

This story reminds us that life's ups and downs aren't set in stone. What seems like a problem today might lead to something good tomorrow, and what looks great now might have its own challenges later on. The key is staying flexible and trusting that things will work out in their own way, helping us face life's twists and turns with greater resilience and acceptance.

Wright Brothers

On December 17, 1903, two brothers from Dayton, Ohio, with no formal engineering training, defied gravity in their curious flying machine over the dunes of North Carolina's remote Outer Banks. By making what many consider the first powered, sustained and controlled manned airplane flights, Orville and Wilbur Wright ushered in the era of flight and soared into history.

Wilbur and Orville were the sons of Milton and Susan Wright and members of a warm, loving family that encouraged learning and doing.

Their dream started with an idea that was planted in their minds by a toy given to them by their father. In the words of the boys, "Late in the autumn of 1878, our father came into the house one evening with some object partly concealed in his hands, and before we could see what it was, he tossed it into the air. Instead of falling to the floor, as we expected, it flew across the room till it struck the ceiling, where it fluttered awhile, and finally sank to the floor." This simple toy made of cork, bamboo and paper and powered by a rubber band mesmerized the boys and sparked their passion for aviation.

The Wright brothers were great thinkers. They enjoyed learning new things. Initially, they recycled broken parts, built a printing press and opened their own printing office. In 1894, Wilbur and Orville were caught up in the bicycling craze that swept the nation. To augment the income from their printing trade, they began repairing and selling bicycles. This soon grew into a full-time business, and in 1896 they began to manufacture their own bikes. The Wright Cycle Company returned a handsome profit, but the brothers cared little about the money. They were already thinking about trading their wheels for wings.

The tight-knit brothers, born four years apart, were wedded to their work; Wilbur told reporters that he didn't have time for both a wife and an airplane.

The brothers spent many hours researching, testing their machines and making improvements after unsuccessful attempts at human flight. What started out as a hobby soon became a passion. With determination and patience, they realized their dream in 1903 when they made the first sustained, controlled flights in a powered aircraft which they named the Wright Flyer.

While the 1903 Wright Flyer did indeed fly, it was underpowered and difficult to control. For two years they made flight after flight, fine tuning the controls, engine, propellers, and configuration of their airplane. At first, they could only fly in a straight line for less than a minute. But by the end of 1905, they were flying figure-eights over Huffman Prairie, staying aloft for over half an hour, or until their fuel ran out. The 1905 Wright Flyer was the world's first practical airplane.

The next time you hear or see an airplane or travel on one, remember where it all started. A simple idea conceived in the minds of two young men who did not finish high school. Believe it or not, they did not have a university degree in Aeronautical Engineering, Mathematics, Physics or any other subject. They were not scientists in the true sense of the word. In fact, many of their peers who did not witness their accomplishment, had trouble believing that two bicycle mechanics from Dayton, Ohio did what they claimed.

The Wright Brothers had a cause and they would not give up; they never let failure or a setback discourage them. When knocked down, they made no excuses; they got back up on their feet and kept going. They epitomized the Samurai saying "Fall seven times and stand up eight". The Wright brothers were models of integrity. Let's learn from them.

Adapted from various versions on the internet.

Ponder this:

The Wright brothers' journey shows us how passion and perseverance can lead to extraordinary achievements. Their accomplishment is particularly inspiring because it defies the conventional image of success - they lacked the prestigious qualifications and formal training typically associated with groundbreaking inventions. Their story reminds us that with unwavering commitment and a strong sense of purpose, even the most ambitious dreams can take flight.

The Value of Time

Imagine there is a bank that credits your account each morning with $86,400.

It carries over no balance from day to day.

Every evening the bank deletes whatever part of the balance you failed to use during the day. What would you do?

Draw out every cent, of course!

Each of us has such a bank. Its name is TIME. Every morning, it credits you with 86,400 seconds.

Every night it writes off, as lost, whatever of this you have failed to invest to good purpose.

It carries over no balance. It allows no overdraft.

Each day it opens a new account for you. Each night it burns the remains of the day.

If you fail to use the day's deposits, the loss is yours. There is no going back.

There is no drawing against the "tomorrow." You must live in the present on today's deposits.

Invest it so as to get from it the utmost in health, happiness, and success!

The clock is running.

To realize the value of *one year*, ask a student who failed a grade. To realize the value of *one month*, ask a mother who gave birth to a premature baby.

To realize the value of *one week*, ask the editor of a weekly newspaper.

To realize the value of *one hour*, ask the lovers who are waiting to meet.

To realize the value of *one minute*, ask a person who missed the train.

To realize the value of *one second*, ask a person who just avoided an accident.

Keep in mind that time waits for no one. Yesterday is history.

Tomorrow is a mystery. Today is a gift.

Make the most of today.

Adapted from various versions on the internet.

Ponder this:

This thought-provoking story presents time as a precious, finite resource. Each day, we are given a symbolic "bank account" of 86,400 seconds – a gift that cannot be carried over or replenished.

The message is clear: make the most of every moment. The past cannot be changed, and the future is uncertain. Today, however, is a gift – an opportunity to invest in our health, happiness, and success. By actively managing our time, we can maximize our return on this precious daily deposit.

Two seeds

Two seeds lay side by side in the fertile soil.

The first seed said, "I want to grow! I want to send my roots deep into the soil beneath me, and thrust my sprouts through the earth's crust above me … I want to unfurl my tender buds like banners to announce the arrival of spring … I want to feel the warmth of the sun on my face and the blessing of the morning dew on my petals!"

And so, she grew…

The second seed said, "Hmmmm. If I send my roots into the ground below, I don't know what I will encounter in the dark. If I push my way through the hard soil above me, I may damage my delicate sprouts… and what if I let my buds open and a snail tries to eat them? And if I were to open my blossoms, a small child may pull me from the ground. No, it is much better for me to wait until it is safe."

And so, she waited…

A yard hen scratching around in the early spring ground for food found the waiting seed and promptly ate it.

(Elan, 2014)

Ponder this:

Life is a constant dance between comfort and growth. This story shows that real growth happens when we step out of our comfort zones. It's okay to be cautious, but being too scared can hold us back. When we grab opportunities and face our fears, life gets brighter and more exciting. Just like a seed breaking through the ground to reach the sun, let's aim high and become our best selves.

The Most Popular vs the Right Decision

This thought experiment, often referred to as the trolley problem, presents a heart-wrenching ethical dilemma. A group of children play near train tracks – some on an operational track and one on a disused one. You, positioned at the track switch, have the horrifying choice of diverting the train to the unused track, sacrificing the lone child, or allowing it to proceed, killing many on the operational track.

Take a pause to think what kind of decision you would make.

The "popular" choice seems clear: sacrifice one life to save many. But the situation is not so black and white. The lone child playing on the unused track arguably made the safe choice, only to be imperiled by the recklessness of the others.

This scenario reflects real-world challenges where the "right" decision can be overshadowed by the will of the majority. In workplaces, communities, and politics, the voices of reason and foresight can be drowned out by popular opinion, no matter how misguided.

Leo Velski Julian, a prominent critic, proposed a different approach. He argued that the children playing on the active track likely understand the danger and would move when they hear the train. Diverting the train, conversely, could endanger the lone child who wouldn't expect a train on the disused track.

Furthermore, the disused track may not be deemed safe for use. Diverting the train could endanger its passengers, introducing a new layer of complexity. The initial decision to save some risks sacrificing hundreds more.

The trolley problem underscores the importance of avoiding hasty judgments. Difficult decisions require careful consideration of all potential consequences. Sometimes, the seemingly popular choice may lead to unintended harm.

Adapted from various versions on the internet.

Ponder this:

When we face tough moral choices, it's important to dig deeper and think about all the possible outcomes. Sometimes, doing what's right might not be what everyone else agrees with, and what everyone likes might not be the best choice morally. But by thinking things through carefully, we can strive to make the most ethical and responsible choice.

Gandhi's Shoes

Mahatma Gandhi, renowned for his non-violent philosophy, displayed remarkable compassion in a seemingly trivial moment. While rushing to board a train, one of his shoes slipped off and fell onto the tracks.

Before anyone could react, Gandhi surprised them all. Instead of retrieving the lost shoe, he swiftly removed the other and flung it back down the tracks, landing it beside its missing partner.

Confused onlookers witnessed this seemingly illogical act. Gandhi's response, however, revealed the depth of his empathy. He explained that by throwing down the second shoe, he ensured that whoever found the first would have a complete pair, a valuable possession for someone less fortunate. In India at that time, a good pair of shoes could represent a significant expense.

This simple act highlights the essence of Gandhi's philosophy.

Adapted from various versions on the internet.

Ponder this:

Compassion isn't just about thinking kind thoughts; it's about taking action when it matters. Gandhi's story shows us how important it is to be on the lookout for chances, no matter how small, to show kindness and help others. Giving, even in unexpected moments, can have a powerful ripple effect that reaches far and wide.

Against All Odds

In 1883, visionary engineer John Roebling dared to dream of a magnificent bridge connecting New York to Long Island. Experts scoffed, declaring it an impossible feat and advised Roebling to forget the idea - it was not practical.

Roebling's conviction was unshakeable. He found an ardent supporter in his son Washington, a rising star in engineering himself. Together, they began translating the dream into reality.

Working together for the first time, the father and son developed concepts of how it could be accomplished and how the obstacles could be overcome. With great excitement and inspiration, and the headiness of a wild challenge before them, they hired their crew and began to build their dream bridge.

The project started well, but when it was only a few months underway a tragic accident on the site took the life of John Roebling leaving his son, Washington Roebling, in charge of the bridge.

Not long after taking charge of the bridge, Washington Roebling suffered a paralyzing injury as well, the result of decompression sickness. So, Washington was left with a certain amount of brain damage, which resulted in him not being able to walk or talk or even move.

That's it! The critics were only waiting for such a thing to happen. They all started…

"We told them so."

"Crazy men and their crazy dreams."

"It's foolish to chase wild visions."

Everyone had a negative comment to make and felt that the project should be scrapped since the Roeblings were the only ones who knew how the bridge could be built. Undeterred, Washington's spirit remained unbroken. Though confined to his bed, he had a burning desire to complete the bridge and his mind was still as sharp as ever.

He tried to inspire and pass on his enthusiasm to some of his friends, but they were too daunted by the task. As he lay on his bed in his hospital room, with the sunlight streaming through the windows, a gentle breeze blew the flimsy white curtains apart and he was able to see the sky and the tops of the trees outside for just a moment.

It seemed that there was a message for him not to give up. Suddenly an idea hit him. All he could do was move one finger and he decided to make the best use of it. By moving this single finger, he slowly developed a code of communication with his wife, Emily.

Through taps on Emily's arm, he painstakingly conveyed instructions to the engineers. For thirteen years, this code served as his lifeline to the project until the bridge was finally completed.

Today the spectacular Brooklyn Bridge stands in all its glory as a tribute to the triumph of one man's indomitable spirit and his determination not to be defeated by circumstances. It is also a tribute to the engineers and their team work, and to their faith in a man who was considered mad by half the world. It stands too as a tangible monument to the love and devotion of his wife who for 13 long years patiently decoded the messages of her husband and told the engineers what to do.

Perhaps this is one of the best examples of a never-say-die attitude that overcomes a terrible physical handicap and achieves an impossible goal.

Often when we face obstacles in our day-to-day life, our hurdles seem very small in comparison to what many others have to face. The Brooklyn Bridge shows us that dreams that seem impossible can be realized with determination and persistence, no matter what the odds.

(Clarita, 2011)

Ponder this:

The Brooklyn Bridge stands not only as an engineering marvel but also as a symbol of steadfast determination. Washington Roebling's story transcends physical limitations. It reminds us that with unwavering resolve, a strong support system, and the courage to keep tapping out our dreams, one tap at a time, we can conquer even the most overwhelming challenges.

Go to the ROAR!

Lions love to eat gazelle meat. But it's very difficult for lions to catch gazelles because the latter run so fast. So instead of trying to catch their quarry, a group of young lions will form a line and try to herd them in a particular direction. The gazelles easily outrun the lions, heading in the opposite direction towards supposed safety.

Except they are unknowingly being steered towards a deep, grassy area where a group of older lions are hiding. The older lions are too old and tired to be part of the chase; many are missing teeth, and would never be able to catch their own meat.

But when the gazelles are driven within close range, the old lions jump up and ROAR loudly. The startled gazelles, responding immediately to a new threat of imminent death, turn and run in the opposite direction. Right back into the mouths of the young lions.

Adapted from various versions on the internet.

Ponder this:

The gazelle's predicament mirrors the challenges we face in our own lives. Fears, both real and imagined, can act as powerful deterrents, prompting us to flee from obstacles and challenges. However, the story reminds us that sometimes, the greatest danger lies not in facing our fears, but in succumbing to them. By confronting our fears head-on, we empower ourselves to overcome obstacles and achieve our goals. The "roar" in our lives may take many forms – a looming deadline, a difficult conversation, a new adventure – but by learning to face them with courage, we emerge stronger and more resilient.

The Power of Perception

In a captivating 2007 social experiment, The Washington Post orchestrated an unexpected performance by world-renowned violinist Joshua Bell. Bell, a virtuoso whose talent commanded packed concert halls and hefty fees, donned a baseball cap and transformed himself into a subway busker. The question at the heart of this experiment: "In a banal setting at an inconvenient time, would beauty transcend?"

For 40 minutes, Bell poured his soul into his music, his Stradivarius violin weaving a tapestry of intricate melodies amidst the hurried commuters at the metro station. Astonishingly, the beauty went largely unnoticed. In fact, out of 1,097 people that passed by Bell, only 27 gave any money, a mere 7 actually stopped and listened for any length of time, and only one person recognized him.

And how much did he make? The violinist who can command thousands for each concert performance on the greatest concert stages in the world made just $52.17, which included $20 from the one person who did recognize him.

Adapted from various versions on the internet.

Ponder this:

The Joshua Bell experiment teaches us a big lesson about how we see the world and the things we might miss in our busy lives. Sometimes, we're so caught up in our daily routines that we overlook the beauty and surprises around us. This story reminds us to slow down, to truly listen, and to appreciate the extraordinary moments that may be hidden in plain sight. When we're more mindful, we discover the incredible richness and wonder that life has to offer.

Don't Waste Your Life

In 1977, a 63-year-old grandmother named Laura Schultz heard screaming from the driveway. Her grandson had been playing with the car and accidentally released the emergency brake. The car rolled onto his arm. She was a petite woman and said she had never lifted a thing over 50 pounds in her life. Yet she lifted the 2,000-pound car off to release her grandson's arm.

After the incident, she was reluctant to speak about it with anyone. After reading her story in the National Enquirer, Dr Charles Garfield, author of Peak Performance managed to obtain an interview with her.

Laura said she didn't like talking about the event because it challenged her beliefs about what she could and could not do. She said, "If I was able to do this when I didn't think I could, what does that say about the rest of my life? Have I wasted it?"

The story has a happy ending. Garfield convinced her that her life wasn't over yet and that she could do whatever she wanted to do. He asked her what her passion was. She said that she had always loved rocks. She wanted to study geology, but her parents could not afford to send both her and her brother to college, so her brother was given preference over her. At 63, with a little coaxing from Charles Garfield, she decided to go back to school to study geology. She eventually got her degree and went to teach at a local community college.

Adapted from various versions on the internet.

Ponder this:

Laura's story teaches us that human potential is often underestimated and unexpressed. We may live for decades, unknowingly harboring hidden capabilities. The narrative challenges us to move beyond self-imposed limitations and embrace the possibility of growth at any stage of life. It's like a wake-up call – to identify our passions, challenge our assumptions, and actively seek a fulfilling existence. That way, when we look back on our lives, we won't wonder "what if?" Laura's journey shows us that it's never too late to discover what we're capable of and write our own amazing story.

True Love - Past, Present and Future

It was about 8:30 am on a busy morning when an elderly gentleman in his 80's arrived to have the stitches removed from his thumb. He stated that he was in a hurry as he had an appointment at 9:00am.

I took his vital signs and had him take a seat, knowing it would be over an hour before someone would be able to attend to him. I saw him looking at his watch and decided, since I was not occupied with another patient, I would take a look at his wound.

On examination, it was well healed, so I talked to one of the doctors and got the necessary materials to remove his sutures and redress his wound.

While taking care of his wound, we engaged in conversation. I enquired if his next appointment was medically related as he was anxious to be on time. He said 'no'; he needed to go to the nursing home to eat breakfast with his wife.

I then inquired about her health. He told me that she had been there for a while and that she had Alzheimer's disease. As I finished dressing his wound, I asked if she would be worried if he was a bit late. He replied that she no longer knew who he was; that she had not recognized him for the past five years.

I was surprised, and asked, "And you still go every morning, even though she doesn't know who you are?"

He smiled as he patted my hand and said, "She doesn't know me, but I still know who she is."

I had to hold back my tears as he left. I had goose bumps on my arm, and thought "That is the kind of love I want in my life."

Adapted from various versions on the internet.

Ponder this:

This story resonates because it speaks to a love that goes beyond the physical. It speaks to a deeper connection, a love that endures through time and circumstance. The man's devotion serves as a powerful reminder that true love is a commitment to the essence of a person, not just a reflection of their current state.

The story compels us to ponder the nature of true love – a love that transcends memory, a love that chooses presence over absence, a love that whispers, "I still know who you are," even when the world forgets.

Schoolyard Fight

This is a true story of an incident in my life as a young boy. At the time, I didn't know I was using visualization to manifest a particular outcome, but this story will give you an understanding of the immense power of visualization combined with emotion.

I think I was in the seventh grade at that time, so I would have been around 11 or 12 years old. In grammar school, like most other schools, we had a bully. His name was Denis Shots.

I'll never forget Denis for as long as I live because, even though we were in the same grade, I couldn't help but think that he was much older than I was. He was huge and probably the only kid in grammar school that already had hair on his chest, and to top it off, he was going a little bald.

Denis was mean and his demeanor showed it. He enjoyed intimidating other kids. Therefore, it's not surprising that I avoided him as much as possible. Besides, I don't have a big stature and I was just a little guy at grammar school.

One day it rained heavily so we remained in the classroom to have lunch. When the teacher left the classroom, Denis decided to make mischief. For some reason, he picked on me. He walked across the room to my desk, pushed me aside, grabbed the brown paper bag that contained my lunch and took it over to the window. Back in those days the schools had old-fashioned crank style windows with big hooks. Denis placed my lunch on the hook and cranked up the window.

Annoyed, I walked over to him. I had a choice. I could try to physically retrieve my lunch bag from him, or I could choose to run out of the classroom and seek some help.

At that moment, I realized that my mother was in the school, working in a room down the hall on a P.T.A. project. Given that I couldn't punch him in the nose and get away with it, I chose the second option. I ran down the hall straight to my mother. She's Portuguese, 100% Portuguese and full of passion. She loves her son very much and I knew she'd fight my battle for me. She didn't let me down. She just tramped right into that classroom with me holding onto her skirt. She went right up to Denis Shots and popped him in the side of the head a few times and got my brown paper bag back for me.

However, that was not the only thing I got back that day. I also got a reputation as being the biggest pansy and sissy that anyone had ever seen in that school.

So, the choice I made that day – to elicit my mother's help instead of standing up for myself – had severe consequences thereafter. I lost all my friends, not that I had many to begin with. Of course, Denis Shots continued to taunt me endlessly.

As the weeks went by, I yearned for an opportunity to redeem myself. Lo and behold, the Universe responded… as it always does. It gave me an opportunity to show that I was not the pansy or sissy that I was perceived to be.

One day, during the morning break in the playground, Denis Shots came up to me and, for no reason at all, pushed me hard. I fell to the ground. As I lay on the ground, I look up at this big chap laughing at me. I realize that unless I did something about it, Denis was going to make my life miserable for the rest of my time at this school. That was unacceptable. Without hesitation, I bounced back up on my feet, got right up to him and pushed him back with all my might. He didn't budge an inch and just laughed at me. Infuriated, close-up with my finger pointed at his face, I said to him, "That's it. I've had enough of you. You and I are going to settle this thing once and for all. I'll meet you after school behind the building."

Holy cow! I couldn't believe what I just did. I challenged Denis Shots to a fight!

This was an absolute mismatch – there was no way in the world that I could beat Denis. I had all day to envision what was going to happen that afternoon. My heart sank just thinking about it, and I couldn't get it out of my mind. The pictures going through my mind were not pleasant. All I could see was pain and more pain. I couldn't concentrate on the remaining lessons for that day. I tried to figure out how I might be able to get out of this fight. Clearly, I was in a fix. I couldn't back out without making an absolute fool of myself. I knew that I had to see this through.

The word got out and started to spread rapidly among the kids. The kids were not very encouraging, to say the least. Mostly, they'd come up to me during the breaks and say, "Hey John, I hear you are taking on Denis Shots after school. Good luck. See you there." I would give them a blank look and then silently say to myself, "Yeah, thanks for reminding me."

However, amidst all my apprehension, something unusual happened – something I wasn't consciously aware of at that time. I started to create another picture… a picture of a world without Denis Shots in it.

I realized that there was no way I could physically beat him, but if I didn't deal with this situation now, it would haunt me for the rest of my life.

So, I said to myself, "I've got to do whatever I need to do to put up with whatever he throws at me. The only way I can 'win' is to show him that I will not quit, no matter how bad he hurts me. I know that if I quit, he'll keep picking on me for weeks and months and years to come. So, I need to show him that, come what may, I will just not quit."

I created a vision of me being beaten, falling down and taking as much punishment as Denis could just dish out. Regardless of what he did, I saw myself getting back up again and again, facing up to him with no sign of quitting. I just played that picture in my mind over and over again. I was so consumed by the impending fight that I didn't pay much attention to any of the lessons in class that day.

Come three o'clock, we all made our way out to the back of the building. There was quite a gathering. Back in those days, there were no formalities. The kids would form a circle around the fighters and the fight would begin. Denis and I squared off immediately.

I did not know it at the time, but visualization works! What happened is exactly what I envisioned. Basically, he was hitting me, and I was hitting the ground. My attempts to strike back were in vain. I couldn't even reach him – I was hitting air. However, no matter how many times he hit me, I kept getting up and going at him with all the strength I could muster.

Now here's the interesting part: When we first started fighting, everybody was rooting for Denis. He was the perceived champion and I was the big sissy.

However, as the fight progressed, a huge shift in energy took place. The more I kept getting up onto my feet – with swollen lips, bleeding nose, bruised hands and knees, torn shirt and soiled pants – the more the kids started rooting for me. Soon enough almost all the kids were rooting for me because they recognized my courage to take on the school bully.

Interestingly, the more the kids rooted for me, the less Denis would hit me and the softer were his blows. It wasn't long before he realized that I wasn't going to give up and that he was being perceived as a villain. To end the fight, he would have to render me helpless and then face the consequences thereafter. It was a no-win situation for him. Common sense prevailed and he held his hands up and said, "John, I quit. I want to be your friend."

I looked at him and said to myself, "What took you so long!" He put his arm around me and that was the beginning of a great friendship. He even became my "bodyguard" throughout my days at high school.

I share this story with you to illustrate that, even at the tender age of twelve, I was able to create a vision that allowed me to push through all the "pain" needed to manifest a favorable outcome.

~ John Kalench (Best-selling author)

Ponder this:

The story highlights the importance of resilience, courage, and perseverance in the face of adversity, showing that even the most daunting situations can be overcome with the right mindset and determination.

Perhaps, a more important lesson in this story is that if you are willing to do your part (i.e. whatever it takes), *the Universe will conspire to help you.*

Too Much Choice

There was an experiment conducted in 1995 by Sheena Iyengar, a professor of business at Columbia University.

In a California gourmet market, Professor Iyengar and her research assistants set up a booth of samples of Wilkin & Sons jams. Every few hours, they switched from offering an assortment of 24 bottles of jam to an assortment of just six bottles of jam. On average, customers tasted two jams, regardless of the size of the assortment, and each one received a coupon good for $1 off one Wilkin & Sons jam.

Here's the interesting part. Sixty percent of customers were drawn to the large assortment, while only 40 percent stopped by the small one. But 30 percent of the people who had sampled from the small assortment decided to buy jam, while only 3 percent of those confronted with the two dozen jams purchased a jar.

Effectively, a greater number of people bought when the assortment size was 6 than when it was 24. That study "raised the hypothesis that the presence of choice might be appealing as a theory, but in reality, people might find more and more choice to actually be debilitating."

Adapted from (Tugend, 2010)

Ponder this:

In a world overflowing with options, from products to careers to life paths, it's easy to feel overwhelmed. This story reminds us that sometimes, less can be more. Limiting our choices can paradoxically lead to greater clarity, satisfaction, and ultimately, better decisions.

The NASA Experiment

Back in the early days of the space program, NASA designed an experiment to determine how its astronauts would cope without gravity, particularly with being upside down in space. NASA needed to know if the environment of space would have some unexpected negative consequences that would endanger the astronauts or their mission.

NASA scientists fitted each of the astronauts with a pair of convex goggles which turned everything they saw upside down. The astronauts had to wear the goggles 24 hours a day, 7 days per week – even when they were asleep.

Although they experienced physical symptoms of anxiety and stress initially, they gradually adapted to their new "realities." On the 26th day of the experiment, something unexpected happened. One of the astronauts was able to see things right-side up again even though he continued to wear the goggles 24 hours a day.

What the scientists discovered is that, between 26-30 days of this continuous stream of new input, one by one, all the astronauts were seeing things the right side-up despite wearing the convex goggles. Basically, each of their brains had formed enough new neural connections to turn this lie into the truth. They had literally re-created their reality!

Then NASA repeated the experiment with a slight change. This time some of the astronauts took the goggles off for a short period of time partway through the experiment. When they put the goggles back on and left them on until the 30th day, their worlds were still upside down, but when they continued on, at 26-30 consecutive days wearing the goggles, the same thing happened – everything was suddenly right-side up again.

What the scientists learned from these experiments is that the brain requires approximately 30 uninterrupted days for new neural connections to form – for new habits to form.

Adapted from various versions on the internet.

Ponder this:

This story offers a powerful message about the potential we hold within our brains. By understanding this potential, we can actively cultivate new, positive habits. Just as the astronauts rewired their perception, we too can shape our reality. By dedicating ourselves to a desired change for a sustained period, we can rewire our brains and pave the way for a more fulfilling life.

What Do You Make?

The dinner guests were sitting around the table discussing life. One man, a CEO, decided to explain the problem with education. He argued: "What's a kid going to learn from someone who decided his best option in life was to become a teacher?"

He said to another guest: "You're a teacher, Susan. Be honest. What do you make?"

Susan, who had a reputation of honesty and frankness, replied, "You want to know what I make?"

"I make kids work harder than they ever thought they could. I can make a C+ feel like the Congressional Medal of Honor and an A- feel like a slap in the face if the student did not do his or her very best."

"You want to know what I make?" "I make kids wonder."

"I make them question." "I make them criticize."

"I make them apologize and mean it." "I make them write."

"I make them read, read, read."

"I make them show all their work in math and hide it all on their final drafts in English."

"I elevate them to experience music and art and the joy in performance, so their lives are rich, full of kindness and culture, and they take pride in themselves and their accomplishments."

"I make them understand that if you have the brains, then follow your heart…and if someone ever tries to judge you by what you make, you pay them no attention."

"You want to know what I make?" "I make a difference."

"By the way, what do you make?"

(Mali, 2011)

Ponder this:

When we talk about jobs, it's easy to focus on how much money they make. But the truth is, the real worth of a job goes way beyond the paycheck. Teachers are an excellent example. Their value isn't just about how much they earn. It's about the incredible impact they have on their students.

Teachers are the architects of future generations. They inspire us to be curious, they make learning exciting, and they help us grow into well-rounded individuals. A great teacher's influence is huge – they shape our lives and lay the groundwork for our success in the long run.

The College Student's Alarming Letter

Dear Mom and Dad,

It's been a while since I left for college, and I apologize for neglecting to write. Life has been busy, but that's no excuse. I should have written sooner.

I'm writing to update you on my college experience so far, but before you get worried, please take a seat. There's no cause for panic, though.

Things haven't been perfect, but I'm coping. The skull fracture and the concussion I got when I jumped out the window of my dormitory when it caught fire shortly after my arrival here is pretty well healed now. I spent only two weeks in the hospital and I can see almost normally now and only get those sick headaches once a day.

Luckily, Butch, a gas station worker near the hostel, saw the fire in the dormitory and my jump from the window. It was Butch who contacted the fire department. He also paid me a visit in the hospital, and because the burnt-out dormitory left me without a place to live, he was gracious enough to extend an invitation for me to move in with him. It's actually a basement room, but even with the clutter, it's still reasonably comfortable.

Butch is a kind guy despite his scruffy appearance, and we intend to get married soon. We haven't set the exact date yet. We are just waiting for his divorce to be finalized; hopefully it will be before my pregnancy begins to show. I know that you are eager to become grandparents someday and would welcome the baby and give it the same love and tender care you gave me as a child.

I hope that you are not upset by my astounding stories. The main reason I'm writing is to explain my grades. My American History

(D) and Chemistry (F) are definitely not what you'd hoped for, and I want you to understand why they're so low. The truth is, I haven't been putting in the effort that I should have. I simply want you to see those marks in their proper perspective.

There's no dramatic story behind my grades. No dorm fire, injuries, hospital stays, weddings, or surprise pregnancies! However, I haven't been applying myself as I should, and that's reflected in my results.

I'm committed to working harder and turning those grades around. I'll keep you updated on my progress.

Love,

Bella

Adapted from various versions on the internet.

Ponder this:

You can put your worries into perspective when you realize that things could be a lot worse than they are. However, in saying that, it's also important to remember that honesty is key in building trust. Even when it's tough, being truthful lays a solid foundation for strong relationships.

Sure, it might seem easier to sugarcoat problems or avoid difficult conversations, but being open and honest leads to better communication. This, in turn, helps us face challenges together and find solutions that benefit everyone. When we're truthful with the people we care about, we invite their support and guidance, which can lead to better outcomes in the end.

The Vasily Alexeev Story

Vasily Alexeev, a Soviet weightlifting legend, was the first to conquer the seemingly insurmountable barrier of lifting 500 pounds. However, his journey to this record-breaking feat was not without its challenges. Alexeev initially plateaued at 499 pounds, convinced it was his absolute limit.

His trainers, determined to shatter this mental barrier, devised a clever ploy. They rigged the barbell to appear as if it held 499 pounds, while secretly loading it with 501.5 pounds. Unaware of the deception, Alexeev lifted the weight with surprising ease.

This seemingly small deception shattered a mental barrier, proving to Alexeev (and the weightlifting world) that 500 pounds was not an impossible feat. Soon thereafter other weight lifters went on to break his record because they now knew it was possible to lift more than 500 pounds.

Adapted from various versions on the internet.

Ponder this:

The story of Vasily Alexeev exemplifies the power of our minds. Often, the limitations we perceive are self-imposed – mental barriers that stop us from reaching our true potential. But by questioning those beliefs and cultivating a mindset of possibility, we can unlock hidden reserves of strength and push beyond what we once thought impossible. Alexeev's story serves as a powerful reminder that sometimes, the greatest weight we lift is the weight of our own doubt.

The Secret to Creating Affluence

This enchanting fable illustrates the mystifying and sometimes elusive workings of the Law of Cause and Effect.

A young man ventured into the forest and approached his spiritual master, with a heartfelt plea: "I yearn for boundless wealth, not for my own sake, but to serve and benefit the world. "What is the secret to wealth?" he inquired.

The wise master replied, "Within every human heart reside two Goddesses: The Goddess of Wealth and the Goddess of Knowledge."

"Although you may hold affection for both, you must devote yourself to one while forsaking the other. Choose one Goddess to pursue. Shower her with love and give her your undivided attention. Having said that, understand that only the Goddess of Wealth can bestow riches upon you. Choose carefully, for you cannot pursue both."

"But, here lies the secret: If you pursue the Goddess of Wealth, she will be pleased with your pursuit, for she delights in being chased. The more you pursue her, the more elusive she becomes. However, should you pursue the Goddess of Knowledge, the Goddess of Wealth will grow intensely jealous and turn her attention towards you. As you seek knowledge, the Goddess of Wealth will seek you. She will never abandon you, showering you with material blessings to win your favor, and the wealth you desire will be yours eternally."

Adapted from (Chopra, 1993)

Ponder this:

The story conveys the counterintuitive idea that focusing on acquiring knowledge, not wealth directly, might lead to unexpected abundance.

The human tendency is to pursue Wealth, which seems like the logical choice. However, wealth is simply an effect, and like any effect, it has a cause. In the fable, pursuing one goddess gets you the best of both worlds; wealth comes from the acquisition and proper application of knowledge.

The Triple-Filter Test

In ancient Greece, Socrates was reputed to hold knowledge in high esteem. One day an acquaintance met the great philosopher and said, "Do you know what I just heard about your friend?"

"Hold on a minute," Socrates replied. "Before you talk to me about my friend, I'd like you to pass a little test. It's called the Triple Filter Test. The first filter is Truth. Have you made absolutely sure that what you are about to tell me is true?"

"Well, no," the man said, "actually I just heard about it and..."

"All right," said Socrates. "So you don't really know if it's true or not. Now, let's try the second filter, the filter of Goodness. Is what you are about to tell me about my friend something good?"

"No, on the contrary..."

"So," Socrates continued, "you want to tell me something bad about him, but you're not certain it's true. You may still pass the test though, because there's one filter left – the filter of Usefulness. Is what you want to tell me about my friend going to be useful to me?"

"No, not really."

"Well," concluded Socrates, "if what you want to tell me is neither true, nor good, nor even useful, why tell it to me at all?"

Adapted from various versions on the internet.

Ponder this:

The Triple-Filter Test story goes beyond the old saying of "if you don't have anything nice to say, don't say it." It teaches us to think before we speak, to choose our words carefully, and to value honesty, kindness, and usefulness in what we say.

When we remember these three filters, we can communicate in a way that's thoughtful and considerate, improving our relationships and creating a more positive atmosphere around us.

SAT Score

This is a true story about a young man from a small town who graduated from high school with straight A's. He then applied to the state university for admission. As part of the admissions procedure, he had to take the Scholastic Aptitude Test, like all the applicants to the universities nationwide. A few weeks later, he received a letter from the admissions department informing him that he scored in the 99th percentile on the test and he was accepted for the fall semester.

He was happy to be accepted but there was one problem. He didn't know about percentiles and he concluded mistakenly that the 99th percentile was his IQ score. He knew that the average IQ is 100 and he felt he could never do university-level work with his 'limited' intelligence.

For the entire fall semester, he failed or nearly failed every course. Finally, his counselor called him in and asked him why he was doing so poorly.

"Well," he said, "You can't blame me. I've only got a 99 IQ."

The counselor had the student's file in front of him. "Why do you say that?" he asked.

"That's what is said in my letter of admission to the university," he replied.

When the counselor realized what had happened, he explained the difference between IQ and a percentile. "A 99th percentile means that you scored equal to or higher than 99 percent of all the students in America who wrote this test. You're one of the brightest kids on the campus."

When the young man realized his error and changed his belief about his intelligence, he became a different person. He went back into his classes and went to work with a new sense of competence and confidence. By the end of the semester he was on the honor roll and he eventually graduated in the top 10 of his class.

(Tracy, 1993)

Ponder this:

This story is like a friendly reminder about how much our beliefs can shape our actions. Most of us act in a way that is congruent with our innermost beliefs – whether we're feeling positive or negative.

The lesson here is pretty cool: the stories we tell ourselves in our heads – like who we think we are and what we think we can achieve – profoundly impact our behavior. So, if we challenge those thoughts that hold us back and start believing in our ability to grow and learn, we can unlock our true potential and achieve remarkable things.

The Fisherman

A boat docked in a tiny Mexican village.

An American tourist complimented the Mexican fisherman on the quality of his fish and asked how long it took him to catch them.

"Not very long," answered the Mexican.

"But then, why didn't you stay out longer and catch more?" asked the American.

The fisherman smiled again and said, "This is plenty here for my family right now. Some of the fish we can eat, and the others we can sell or trade for the other things we need."

"But it's not even lunchtime. What do you do with the rest of your time?"

"In the morning," the fisherman explained, "I like to sleep late. When I wake, I fish a little, mostly just for the pleasure of fishing. In the afternoon, I play with my children and take a siesta with my wife. In the evenings, I have dinner with my family. And then, when my children are sleeping, I stroll into the village, where I sip wine and play guitar with my friends."

The American scoffed and said, "I'm a Harvard MBA and I can help you."

The fisherman was a little skeptical, but nonetheless he obliged and asked, "How?"

"You should fish longer every day," the American counseled, "late into the afternoon. This way you will catch more fish and make more money, and you can buy a bigger boat. With the bigger boat, you will catch even more fish, make even more money, and then you can buy another boat and hire another man to work the second boat."

"But what then?" the fisherman inquired.

"Oh, we are just getting started! With two boats, you'll catch even more fish and make even more money, and before you know it, you'll have a whole fleet of boats and every man in the village looking for work will come to you."

"But what then?" the fisherman asked.

"Before too long, you can cut out the middleman, sell your fish directly to the cannery, and make more money. As your fleet of boats continues to expand, you can build your own cannery. And before you know it, you'll be able to leave this small coastal village, move to Mexico City, and manage your expanding enterprise."

"But what then?" the fisherman persisted.

"Well then, you can begin to ship your fish to different parts of the world. Down into Asia and Australia and up into North America. And as demand grows for your fish, you can leave Mexico City, move to Los Angeles, open a distribution plant there, and begin to ship your fish to Europe and every corner of the globe."

"But what then?" the fisherman asked again.

The American continued, "By then, your business will be one of the great ventures of the industry. You can move to New York City and manage your empire from the epicenter of the business world."

"How long will all this take?" the fisherman asked. "Twenty-five, maybe thirty years," the banker explained.

"But what will I do then?" the fisherman asked.

The American's eyes lit up like a Christmas tree. "That's the best part," he said. "When the time is just right, you can go down to

Wall Street, list your business as a public company, offer an IPO, and make millions and millions of dollars."

"Millions?" the fisherman asked.

"More money than you ever dreamed you could earn in ten lifetimes," the American explained.

"But what then?" the fisherman asked.

The American did not know what to say. He had reached his climax. He was stumped. But then a thought crossed his mind and triggered an idea, and he turned once more to the fisherman and spoke.

"Well then, you could move to a small coastal village... You could sleep late... You could fish just for the pleasure of fishing... In the afternoons, you could take a siesta with your wife... In the evenings, you could have dinner with your family... and then you could stroll into the village and sip wine and play guitar and sing songs with your friends..."

Adapted from various versions on the internet.

Ponder this:

While success has its rewards, sometimes we need to put our work into perspective and see the bigger picture.

The story encourages us to *critically examine the motivations behind our own aspirations.* It prompts us to ask ourselves: *What truly defines success for me?* Are we chasing an externally imposed definition of success, or are we pursuing goals that align with our core values and contribute to our overall well-being?

The Praying Hands

Back in the fifteenth century, in a tiny village near Nuremberg, lived a family with eighteen children. Eighteen! In order merely to keep food on the table for this big family, the father and head of the household, a goldsmith by profession, worked almost eighteen hours a day at his trade and any other paying chore he could find in the neighborhood.

Despite their seemingly hopeless condition, two of Albrecht Durer's children had a dream. They both wanted to pursue their talent for art, but they knew full well that their father could never afford to send either of them to Nuremberg to study at the Academy.

After many long discussions at night in their crowded bed, the two boys finally worked out a pact. They would toss a coin. The loser would go down into the nearby mines and, with his earnings, support his brother while he attended the academy. Then, when that brother who won the toss completed his studies, in four years, he would support the other brother at the academy, either with sales of his artwork or, if necessary, also by laboring in the mines.

They tossed a coin on a Sunday morning after church. Albrecht Durer won the toss and went off to Nuremberg.

Albert went down into the dangerous mines and, for the next four years, financed his brother, whose work at the academy was almost an immediate sensation. Albrecht's etchings, his woodcuts, and his oils were far better than those of most of his professors, and by the time he graduated, he was beginning to earn considerable fees for his commissioned works.

When the young artist returned to his village, the Durer family held a festive dinner on their lawn to celebrate Albrecht's triumphant homecoming. After a long and memorable meal, punctuated with music and laughter, Albrecht rose from his honored position at the head of the table to drink a toast to his beloved brother for the years of sacrifice that had enabled Albrecht to fulfil his ambition. His closing words were, "And now, Albert, blessed brother of mine, now it is your turn. Now you can go to Nuremberg to pursue your dream, and I will take care of you."

All heads turned in eager expectation to the far end of the table where Albert sat, tears streaming down his pale face, shaking his lowered head from side to side while he sobbed and repeated, over and over, "No ...no ...no ...no."

Finally, Albert rose and wiped the tears from his cheeks. He glanced down the long table at the faces he loved, and then, holding his hands close to his right cheek, he said softly, "No, brother. I cannot go to Nuremberg. It is too late for me. Look ... look what four years in the mines have done to my hands! The bones in every finger have been smashed at least once, and lately I have been suffering from arthritis so badly in my right hand that I cannot even hold a glass to return your toast, much less make delicate lines on parchment or canvas with a pen or a brush. No, brother... for me it is too late."

More than 450 years have passed. By now, Albrecht Durer's hundreds of masterful portraits, pen and silver point sketches, watercolors, charcoals, woodcuts, and copper engravings hang in every great museum in the world, but the odds are great that you, like most people, are familiar with only one of Albrecht Durer's works. More than merely being familiar with it, you very well may have a reproduction hanging in your home or office.

One day, to pay homage to Albert for all that he had sacrificed, Albrecht Durer painstakingly drew his brother's abused hands with palms together and thin fingers stretched skyward. He called his powerful drawing simply "Hands," but the entire world almost immediately opened their hearts to his great masterpiece and renamed his tribute of love "The Praying Hands."

(Mandino, 1990)

Ponder this:

This story goes beyond just artistic dreams. It's about something we all experience: needing a helping hand to reach our goals. We are all indebted, in some way, to the support we receive from friends, family, mentors, and even complete strangers throughout our lives. The Praying Hands story serves as a powerful call to acknowledge and express gratitude for those who have helped us on our journeys.

Chaser: The Wonder Dog

Following his retirement from Wofford College, psychologist John W. Pilley, encouraged by his family, sought companionship in a canine companion. He brought home a Border Collie puppy, whom he named Chaser. Their journey together began in 2004.

Starting from Chaser's puppyhood, Pilley embarked on a unique training method. He would introduce new toys, repeating their names up to 40 times, and then hide them for the playful pup to find.

Through this dedicated training, Chaser astoundingly memorized the names of over 1,000 toys, even categorizing them by function and shape. On a talk show, Pilley downplayed Chaser's exceptional memory as characteristic of the intelligent Border Collie breed. However, he emphasized that everything she learned came from positive reinforcement through play, particularly with her beloved blue racquet ball.

"She demands four to five hours of training daily," Pilley once said with a chuckle, then 82 years old, "I have to go to bed just to get away from her!"

While Chaser was Pilley's research partner from her infancy, she was first and foremost a cherished member of the family. Affectionately known as "the world's smartest dog," Chaser passed away in 2019 at the age of 15.

Adapted from various versions on the internet.

Ponder this:

The story of Chaser, the "world's smartest dog," beautifully illustrates the power of dedication and positive reinforcement in unlocking potential. Her owner, Pilley, was super dedicated to teaching Chaser through fun games. And, it worked like magic!

Not only did Chaser become super smart, but Pilley's patience and positive approach fostered a deep and loving bond between them.

This heartwarming story teaches us a valuable lesson for our own lives too. With a little patience, staying consistent, and focusing on positive rewards, we can achieve remarkable success – not just in training pets but in anything we set our minds to!

The Black Dot

Professor Harrison handed out the test papers with the writing facing down, as is customary. When everyone got their papers, he told them to turn them over. Instead of questions, there was just one black dot in the middle of the white paper.

The students were confused. What were they supposed to do with this dot? Was it a test of their drawing skills or a hidden puzzle?

The professor, seeing the expression on everyone's faces, gave them the following instruction: "This test paper represents life. Write about what you see there."

Even though they were puzzled, they started writing. Some speculated about the dot's origin and what it represented, while others analyzed its placement. A few students even got deep into thinking about life's imperfections.

After the class ended, Professor Harrison collected the papers and stood in front of the students. He read each answer out loud. Surprisingly, every student had focused on the black dot, trying to figure out its meaning.

Finally, the room got quiet as Professor Harrison spoke to the students:

"I won't give you grades for this. Instead, think about the lesson here. Notice that none of you talked about the big, white space – the untouched part around the dot. This happens in life too. We worry about the black dots – like health problems, money issues, bad relationships, and disappointments. Even though these problems are small compared to all the good things in life, they can make us feel bad."

He looked around the room to make his point clear. "Change your focus. Look at the white spaces – the happy moments, love, and simple joys. Forget about the black dots that make you sad. Be thankful and live a happy life filled with blessings."

And so, the students left the class with a new way of thinking. They promised to see beyond the dots – to cherish the expansive canvas of life and find happiness in its unblemished spaces

Adapted from various versions on the internet.

Ponder this:

Professor Harrison's unique test offers a powerful reflection on our tendency to fixate on the negative stuff - like a bad grade, money concern, or relationship matter – represented by the black dot. But here's the thing: that tiny black dot is just a small part of the whole picture. The rest of the paper? That's the good stuff – supportive friends, fun experiences, and triumphs both big and small.

Professor Harrison's point is that we often forget to appreciate the "white space" in our lives. By focusing on the good stuff, expressing gratitude for the things we have, we don't just feel happier, we might even find it easier to deal with the challenges (the black dots) that come our way.

Think about it: happiness isn't about having a perfect life with no problems. It's about being able to see the good things, even when things are tough. So, next time you see a black dot, remember the white space. And maybe, just maybe, you'll find a little more happiness along the way.

Liar... Get out of here!

A small frog, born and raised in a deep, mossy well, had never known anything different. Bound by the well's walls, he couldn't conceive another kind of life and felt no desire for anything more.

One sunny day, a frog from a nearby lake tumbled into the well. Excited by the unexpected visitor, the little frog inquired, "Where do you come from?"

"I come from the lake," the fallen frog replied.

"The lake!" exclaimed the little frog, leaping across the well's breadth. "How big is it? As big as my well?"

"My friend," the lake frog cautioned, "your well is no match for the vastness of the lake."

Unfazed, the little frog leaped again. "Is your lake this big?"

Taken aback, the lake frog exclaimed, "Nonsense! The lake is thousands of times larger than this well. And there's a whole world above you that you can't even imagine!"

The little frog scoffed. "Rubbish! Nothing can be bigger or better than my well."

He then hollered, "Liar! Get out of here!"

Adapted from various versions on the internet.

Ponder this:

Our understanding of the world mostly comes from what we see, taste, touch, smell, and hear – our five senses. But here's the thing: our senses have limits, so our view of the world is also limited. That's not a big deal, unless we start thinking that what we've experienced is the only truth. Spoiler alert: it's not! None of us knows everything; we're all clueless about something – it's just different things for each of us.

Now, with respect to this story, it shows us how having a narrow mind and ignoring experiences different from ours can be a problem. The little frog's inability to imagine a world beyond his well demonstrates the importance of being open-minded and ready to learn from others.

Change or Die – South American Tribe

In the study of a native tribe in South America it was found that the people in the tribe had been dying prematurely from a strange illness for many generations. Scientists finally discovered that the disease was carried by an insect that lived in the walls of their clay homes. The natives had several options:

1. They could destroy the insects with a pesticide.
2. They could tear down and rebuild their homes.
3. They could move to a new location where the insects weren't found.
4. They could do nothing and continue to die young, just as they had for generations.

Incredibly, they chose to do nothing, and simply be victims of circumstances. They took the path of least effort and no change, and paid the price with their lives.

(Waitley, 1992)

Ponder this:

When faced with a problem, it is important to take action and make changes to overcome it. Change can be difficult and uncomfortable, but it is often necessary for survival and growth. This story reminds us that sometimes we need to step out of our comfort zones and embrace change in order to thrive.

How Would You Like to be Remembered?

Imagine flipping open the morning paper, and there, staring back at you from the obituary page, is your own name. A cruel twist of fate, a case of mistaken identity announcing your demise. You're not dead...yet. Relief washes over you, but then, a chilling thought creeps in. How would you be remembered?

The obituary paints a grim picture of you – a life dedicated to destruction; a "merchant of death" who had grown rich by developing new ways to "mutilate and kill" more people more quickly than anyone else who had ever lived.

This was the wake-up call for Alfred Nobel, the inventor of dynamite. When his brother Ludvig died from a heart attack in 1888, a newspaper ran a long obituary of Alfred Nobel, believing that it was he who had passed away. Thus, Alfred Nobel had an opportunity granted to few people: to read his obituary while alive.

He was appalled by what he read. "A legacy of violence. Is this all I'll leave behind?" he whispered, the newspaper suddenly feeling heavy in his hands.

At that moment, Alfred Nobel realized two things: that this was how he was going to be remembered, and that this was not how he wanted to be remembered.

From that day forward, Alfred Nobel embarked on a mission to redefine his story, transforming his fortune into a celebration of peace, of progress, of the very things his invention so brutally threatened. He became Alfred Nobel, the Nobel Prize founder, his name forever etched in the annals of humanity's advancement, not its destruction.

What about you?

What whispers will follow you when you're gone? Will loved ones speak of your kindness, your humor, your unwavering support? Or will they recount a life spent chasing things, a life that left little impact on the world around you?

This isn't about fancy cars or a bulging bank account. The truth is, your legacy is being written right now. Every decision, every action, creates the fabric of your legacy. It's the kindness you offer, the knowledge you share, the love you leave behind. Will you be remembered as a footnote, or a force for good? The choice is yours.

Adapted from various versions on the internet.

Ponder this:

Alfred Nobel's story is a powerful reminder that our legacies are not set in stone. Nobel's awakening to how he was perceived as the "merchant of death" highlights the power of self-reflection and the ability to change one's legacy. It teaches us that our actions and values define how we are remembered and encourages us to align our lives with what we wish to leave behind as our legacy.

So, what's the lesson here? It's never too late to rewrite your story. Whether you're a scientist, an artist, or just a regular person, your choices matter. You can leave behind something meaningful – a legacy that reflects your most authentic self and contributes meaningfully to the world around you. For most of us, our legacy is the most important thing that we leave behind. Make yours memorable.

Consider this… as an add-on to your legacy:
Imagine the impact of sharing this book with someone you care about - a friend, family member, or partner. Your simple gesture could spark a life-changing transformation, not just for them but for everyone they inspire. Imagine the ripple effect – a single act of generosity can set in motion a cascade of inspiration… all because you cared to share. *Isn't that a legacy worth creating?*

The Thriving Newspaper Stand

In New York City, just fifteen yards from another stand, a particular newspaper vendor consistently outsold its neighbor by a staggering four times. The secret? Gratitude. After every sale, the owner of the thriving stand offered a simple yet powerful expression: "Thank you." This genuine gratitude drew customers in, willing to go out of their way to patronize a stand where they felt recognized and valued.

Adapted from various versions on the internet.

Ponder this:

According to research, expressing gratitude can actually enhance happiness and well-being. This is a remarkable finding. The benefits, though, go beyond contentment with oneself. The thriving newspaper stand is positive proof that expressing gratitude may improve business results.

A Lesson in Faith and Trust

Fueled by a desire for solo glory, an ambitious mountain climber embarked on a perilous ascent. As dusk painted the sky, he neared the summit, his determination battling the encroaching darkness.

Tragically, a misstep sent him plummeting down the rocky slopes. His life flashed before him in those agonizing moments, the chilling realization of imminent death settling in.

Suddenly, a jolt halted his descent. He dangled precariously, suspended by a safety rope. In desperation, a prayer escaped his lips, pleading for divine intervention. A powerful voice boomed from above, echoing through the vastness: "What would you have me do?"

"Save me!" the climber cried out; his voice laced with urgency.

"Do you truly believe I can?" the voice queried.

"Of course, my Lord!" he affirmed; his faith seemingly unwavering.

Then came the unexpected instruction: "Cut the rope if you wish to be saved."

Silence descended, thick and heavy. The climber, caught in a web of fear and doubt, clung desperately to the very lifeline he was instructed to sever.

The following morning, a rescue team found the climber frozen to death, his hands still gripping the rope mere inches above the ground.

Adapted from various versions on the internet.

Ponder this:

This story provides a powerful illustration of how faith and trust can be really complicated. It prompts us to reflect on the discrepancy between *professing faith and truly embodying it through action.*

While the story does not advocate for blind faith or a disregard for personal responsibility, it does invite us to contemplate the depth and authenticity of our faith. Ultimately, it serves as a reminder that true faith requires a willingness to surrender and trust, even when it feels counterintuitive.

Basketball Experiment

Visualization plays a key role in the successes of many great athletes. Physiologist Edmund Jacobson found that when he had subjects visualize certain athletic activities, amazingly it affected and sharpened their muscles. He discovered subtle but very real movements in the muscles that corresponded to the movement the muscles would make if they were really performing the imagined activity.

Further research revealed that a person who consistently visualizes a certain physical skill develops "muscle memory" which helps him when he physically engages in the activity. A related study by Australian psychologist Alan Richardson confirmed the reality of the phenomenon.

Richardson chose three groups of students at random. None had ever practised visualization. The first group practised free throws every day for twenty days. The second made free throws on the first day and the twentieth day, as did the third group. But members of the third group spent 20 minutes every day visualizing free throws. If they "missed," they "practised" getting the next shot right.

On the twentieth day Richardson measured the percentage of improvement in each group. The group that practised daily improved 24 percent. The second group, unsurprisingly, improved not at all. The third group, which had physically practised no more than the second, did twenty-three percent better – almost as well as the first group!

In his paper on the experiment, published in Research Quarterly, Richardson wrote that the most effective visualization occurs when the visualizer feels and sees what he is doing. In other words, the visualizers in the basketball experiment "felt" the ball in their hands and "heard" it bounce, in addition to "seeing" it go through the hoop.

(Randolph, 2002)

Ponder this:

The story goes beyond sports and shows us how powerful our minds can be. Did you know that our brains can't tell the difference between real actions and vivid imagination? That's where visualization comes in. It's not just daydreaming; it's like practicing in your mind, which can actually make you better at things in real life. When we visualize with all our senses and feelings, we're training our brains (by creating neural pathways that prepare us) to succeed in anything we set our minds to.

Shake It Off and Step Up

One day a farmer's mule fell into a well. The animal cried piteously for hours as the farmer tried to figure out a way to get him out.

The well was deep and the mule was heavy. The farmer certainly did not have the resources to lift the animal out. Finally, he decided the mule was too old and the unused well needed to be covered anyway, so he would bury the mule in the well and, in that way, solve two problems at the same time.

He immediately enlisted his neighbors to help him cover up the well and put the mule out of his misery. They all grabbed shovels and began throwing dirt into the well. At first, the mule realized what was happening and became hysterical. Soon, to everyone's amazement, he quieted down. It suddenly dawned upon him that every time a shovel load of dirt landed on him, he should shake it off and step up! So, with every shovel of dirt that hit his back, the mule would shake it off and step up.

Eventually, to everyone's amazement, the old mule, exhausted and dirty, but very much alive, stepped up over the edge of the well and trotted off!

Adapted from various versions on the internet.

Ponder this:

Life, like the dirt raining down on the mule, is bound to throw challenges our way. It's easy to succumb to despair, to wallow in our problems like the initially frantic mule. The key takeaway from this story lies in the mule's remarkable shift in perspective. By viewing each obstacle as an opportunity to rise above, rather than a burden to be endured, we can transform difficulties into stepping stones on our path to success. Just like the mule, we can emerge from adversity stronger, more resourceful, and empowered to face whatever life throws our way.

Whining Dog

A young woman strolled down the street when she noticed an elderly man sitting on his porch with his dog whining persistently. Intrigued by the incessant noise, she stopped and inquired, "Excuse me, sir, but why is your dog whining so?"

The man replied calmly, "He's sitting on a nail."

Surprised, the woman asked, "Then why doesn't he just get up?"

The man offered a simple yet profound answer: "Because it doesn't hurt enough yet."

Adapted from various versions on the internet.

Ponder this:

The story offers a valuable lesson in taking action to change our circumstances. It highlights that sometimes we tolerate discomfort or inconvenience, even if it hinders us. The key takeaway is to be proactive in addressing challenges. Don't wait for the "pain" to become unbearable before taking steps towards improvement.

Fleas in a Jar

Fleas are astonishing jumpers, capable of leaping over 150 times their own height. In an experiment, a scientist placed several fleas in a glass jar. Unsurprisingly, they quickly jumped out. The scientist then returned the fleas to the jar and covered it with a glass lid. Initially, the fleas jumped freely, hitting the lid and falling back down. After a while, however, they adapted their behavior. Conditioned by the presence of the lid, they began jumping to a lower height to avoid hitting it.

One might argue the fleas were being clever, learning to avoid a futile endeavor.

However, the true test came when the scientist removed the lid entirely. Despite the newfound freedom, the fleas continued jumping at their self-imposed "safe" height. They had become accustomed to the limitation and, in a sense, internalized it. The jar remained their prison, not because of the physical barrier, but because of their conditioned behavior.

Adapted from various versions on the internet.

Ponder this:

The fleas in the jar represent individuals who have been conditioned to believe they are limited by external circumstances. They adapt to their restricted environment, even when the limitations are removed. This story serves as a metaphor for learned helplessness.

Just like the fleas, we can become conditioned by limitations, both real and imagined. This story is a reminder that we shouldn't let imaginary limits stop us from reaching our full potential. By challenging our assumptions and pushing past our self-imposed boundaries, we might surprise ourselves with what we can achieve.

The Hundredth Monkey Phenomenon

The Japanese monkey, Macaca fuscata, had been observed in the wild for a period of over thirty years.

In 1952, on the island of Koshima, scientists were providing monkeys with sweet potatoes dropped in the sand. The monkeys liked the taste of the raw sweet potatoes, but they found the dirt unpleasant. An 18-month-old female (named Imo) found she could get rid of the sand by washing the potatoes in a nearby stream. She taught this trick to her mother and her playmates; they taught their mothers, too.

This cultural innovation was gradually picked up and between 1952 and 1958 all the young monkeys learned to wash the sandy sweet potatoes to make them more palatable. Only the adults who imitated their children learned this social improvement. Other adults kept eating the dirty sweet potatoes.

One day in 1958, something interesting happened. A certain number of Koshima monkeys were washing sweet potatoes. The exact number is not known. Let's assume that there were 99 monkeys washing potatoes. Let's further assume that later that morning, the hundredth monkey learned to wash potatoes.

Then a most amazing phenomenon occurred!

By that evening almost every monkey in the tribe was washing sweet potatoes before eating them. The added energy of this hundredth monkey somehow created an ideological breakthrough!

But it didn't end there. A most surprising thing observed by these scientists was that the monkeys' habit of washing sweet potatoes then jumped across the sea.

Colonies of monkeys on other islands and the mainland troop of monkeys at Takasakiyama began washing their sweet potatoes too!

Thus, when a certain critical number achieves an awareness, this new awareness may be communicated from mind to mind. Although the exact number may vary, this Hundredth Monkey Phenomenon means that when only a limited number of people know of a new way, it may remain the conscious property of these people. But there is a point at which, if only one more person tunes-in to a new awareness, an energy field is strengthened so that this awareness is picked up by almost everyone!

(The Hundredth Monkey Phenomenon, 2009)

Ponder this:

The Hundredth Monkey Phenomenon compels us to consider the dynamics of collective learning. It suggests that ideas and behaviors can spread not just through direct communication, but also through a kind of shared consciousness. Even more fascinating is the idea that monkeys on different islands mysteriously started engaging in this new behavior, despite there being no physical barriers between them. To some extent it makes sense when we consider that everything is energy and we are all an integral part of this matrix of universal energy, interconnected in some way.

The Sweeter Apple

A little girl, clutching two apples, looked up as her mother entered the room. A warm smile on her face, the mother asked, "Sweetheart, would you be willing to share one of your apples with me?"

The girl, quick as a flash, took a bite from each apple, one after the other. The mother's smile faltered, but she tried to mask her disappointment.

Just then, the girl held out one of the bitten apples. "Here you go, Mommy," she offered. "This one is the sweeter one."

The mother, touched by her daughter's gesture, felt a pang of remorse for her initial judgment. A broader smile returned to her face, realizing her daughter, in her innocent way, had wanted to share the better apple.

This simple story serves as a gentle reminder to pause before jumping to conclusions. Appearances can be deceiving, and true intentions often lie beneath the surface.

Adapted from various versions on the internet.

Ponder this:

The story imparts the wisdom of pausing before making judgments. It encourages us to cultivate patience in our interactions with others and consider others' feelings before acting impulsively. By waiting and observing, we may discover genuine kindness and generosity that are not immediately apparent.

A Leader Always Fails Upwards!

Abraham Lincoln's rise to the presidency is a testament to his remarkable character. Born in a log cabin, he went on to lead the United States through its most turbulent period. The challenges of achieving leadership in the mid-19th century were significant. While stories abound of individuals like Lincoln, Andrew Jackson, and Ulysses S. Grant rising from humble beginnings, they were the exception, not the rule. Success typically favored those with advantages. Financial mobility was far more limited, and recovering from setbacks was a much steeper climb. Social safety nets were nonexistent, leaving individuals to fend for themselves.

Considering these challenges, let's examine some of the obstacles Lincoln faced and overcame. You've likely encountered similar lists detailing his failures, but revisiting them is crucial. As you read, reflect on your own setbacks and how you responded.

In 1832, Lincoln was working in a general store in Illinois when he decided to run for the state legislature. However, the election was some months away, and before it took place, the general store went bankrupt and Lincoln was out of a job. So, he joined the army and served three months. When he got out, it was time for the election – which he lost.

Undeterred, Lincoln partnered to open a new store. Unfortunately, his partner embezzled funds, leading to bankruptcy. The partner then died, leaving Lincoln with debts that took years to repay.

Despite these setbacks, Lincoln persevered. In 1834, he successfully ran for state legislature, serving four consecutive terms. This period, however, was also marked by significant emotional struggles, what today might be diagnosed as clinical depression.

By 1836, Lincoln had become a licensed attorney. At that time, a law degree was not required to pass the bar exam, and Lincoln had been studying on his own for years. He later became a circuit- riding lawyer, traveling from county to county in Illinois to plead cases in different jurisdictions. He was known for his diligence, missing only two court sessions on the circuit between 1849 and 1860.

Lincoln's political ambitions continued, though not without setbacks. He faced defeats in 1838 for Speaker of the Illinois legislature and in 1843 for a congressional nomination. In 1846, he was elected to Congress, but term limits forced him out in 1848. He lost a Senate bid in 1854, the vice-presidential nomination in 1856, and another Senate race in 1858.

Yet, in spite of these numerous defeats, 1860 saw him become President of the United States. Notably, Lincoln's failures were often followed by attempts at even higher office. After losing his state legislature seat, he ran for Congress. Following a failed Senate bid, he pursued the vice presidency. And after another Senate defeat, he ultimately became president.

Lincoln saw himself as a leader long before anyone else did. This self-assuredness was the cornerstone of his leadership genius. While he encountered many failures, he somehow always "failed upwards." He was propelled by a sense of mission, and he was willing and able to do whatever it took to get that great mission accomplished.

Adapted from a narrative by Dr. Tony Alessandra

Ponder this:

The path to success is littered with the fallen who lacked the tenacity to persevere through repeated failures. Look at Lincoln – he faced plenty of failures but never gave up. His story teaches us something timeless: how to bounce back from setbacks. By embracing the concept of "failing upwards," we can transform setbacks into opportunities for growth and reach our full potential. Success is not the absence of failure; it's the ability to learn, adapt, and rise stronger after each challenge.

Carrying in the mind

Two traveling monks reached a river where they met a young woman. Wary of the current, she asked if they could carry her across. One of the monks hesitated, but the other quickly picked her up onto his shoulders, transported her across the water, and put her down on the other bank. She thanked him and departed.

As the monks continued on their way, the one was brooding and preoccupied. Unable to hold his silence, he spoke out. "Brother, our spiritual training teaches us to avoid any contact with women, but you picked that one up on your shoulders and carried her!"

"Brother," the second monk replied, "I set her down on the other side, while you are still carrying her."

Adapted from a traditional tale.

Ponder this:

The parable teaches us about the dangers of holding onto negative thoughts and emotions. Just like the second monk who set the woman down on the other side of the river and moved on, we should learn to let go of our negative thoughts and emotions and not let them weigh us down. By doing so, we can live a more peaceful and fulfilling life.

Heaven and Hell

One day a conflicted Samurai was meandering down a dirt road. He was unkempt, dishevelled and nursing a hangover. Right when he was at the depths of his depression, he noticed a monk approaching. The closer the monk got, the clearer it became that the monk knew holy secrets. When the monk passed, the Samurai spoke up.

"Holy monk, I seek your guidance. I am depressed as I do not know what awaits me after this life. Please, can you tell me the difference between Heaven and Hell?"

The monk returned a look of disgust and said, "You are but a lonely, shameful Samurai. You kill with no mercy; your sword is rusty and you have nothing to offer the world. Why should I share such holy secrets with such a despicable man?"

Outraged, the Samurai unsheathed his sword. He had never experienced such anger, and he decided to strike down this secret-hoarding monk. He raised his sword and brought it down over the monk's head. Just before contact, without flinching, the monk smiled.

"This is Hell. You have given into anger and you are now possessed by it."

Realizing the lesson he just learned, a sense of remorse and humility came over him. He was ashamed by his actions. He immediately cast aside his sword and fell to his knees.

"Holy monk, please forgive me for my actions. I am unworthy of your presence. I will never raise my sword in anger again."

Smiling, the monk replied, "This, my dear Samurai, is Heaven. You are humble, and soon serenity will envelope you."

Adapted from various versions on the internet.

Ponder this:

In life, we often talk about Heaven and Hell as places we might go after we're done here. But they're also states of mind that we experience throughout our lives. Some folks, like the conflicted Samurai, go through life feeling like they're stuck in Hell, always waiting for Heaven to show up, not realizing it's already within their grasp.

By being kind, humble, and aware of ourselves and others, we can discover our own piece of Heaven and live a truly satisfying life.

Lessons From a Snow Globe

Have you ever seen a snow globe?

It generally has a picturesque scene with pretty houses and neat roads. Shake it and it grows hazy as if snow was falling. I saw a good snow globe once where it took hours for the 'snow' to settle and the houses to be visible again.

Hold that scene in mind. I will come back to it and the other observations I am about to make and tie them all together.

Mark Twain supposedly said, "It's not the things you don't know that kill you. It's the things you know that just ain't so."

This is a profound, deeply penetrating observation.

When I came to Columbia to do my Ph.D. I made a friend. Her father was the CEO of a Fortune 250 company, and she owned a substantial chunk of it herself. She was intelligent and sophisticated. She saw films like *The Garden of the Finzi-Continis* and by directors like Bertolucci and Costa-Gavras and Bergman. She had seen more Satyajit Ray movies than I had. She went to wine tastings, the Opera, art museums, concerts and the theater. She hung out with friends in hot new bars and checked out new restaurants.

That, I thought, was what life should be like and she was living it to the fullest. I could not keep up and dropped out of her circle regretfully.

I became an executive in an entertainment conglomerate and did well. My calendar started to fill up but not to the extent of my erstwhile friend. I had an uncle and aunt who came from modest circumstances and lived quietly. I offered to take them out or send them on trips, but they declined politely. They had never left the village in which they were born and knew nothing of the world outside. They told me that they were quite satisfied and didn't need anything.

I felt sorry for them. How sad to live a life so circumscribed and ignorant of what was happening in the broader world.

It took me decades to realize that I was the fool.

Frenetic activity does nothing but generate mental chatter that quickly spins out of control. It is just like shaking and shaking the snow globe and it takes a very long time for the haze to settle. What I thought was an ideal life, a life that I tried to show others, was simply a vortex of agitations that would not let me be. Mark Twain was dead on. What I 'knew' just wasn't so.

Think of your life. How much of your activity – the quest for entertainment, the social obligations, the 'must do' experiences – is simply a way by which your mind gets diverted into channels that do not allow it to rest and be quiescent? How much of it is shaking the snow globe?

What will you do to eliminate this and bring tranquillity back into your life?

(Rao, Prof. Srikumar - https://theraoinstitute.com)

Ponder this:

The author encourages readers to reflect on their lives and the choices they make.

The idea is to focus on what truly matters in life and avoid getting caught up in the pursuit of material success and external validation. Instead, we should strive to find inner peace and tranquillity by eliminating frenetic activity and embracing a more mindful and reflective approach to life.

A Pound of Butter

A farmer regularly sold a pound of butter to a baker. One day, suspecting he was shorted, the baker weighed the butter and found it was much less than a pound. Infuriated, he dragged the farmer to court.

The judge, addressing the farmer, inquired, "Do you have a proper scale to measure the butter?"

The farmer, a simple man, replied, "Your Honor, I'm afraid not. But I do have a balance scale."

Intrigued, the judge asked, "And how, exactly, did you weigh the butter using a balance scale?"

The farmer, with a knowing smile, explained, "Well, Your Honor, for much longer than I've been selling butter to this baker, I've been buying a loaf of bread from him, a pound loaf, mind you. Every day, when the baker delivers the bread, I place it on the scale and give him back the same weight in butter. So, if anyone's to be blamed for a shortage, it surely can't be me!"

This simple story cleverly highlights the importance of fairness and using a consistent standard for measurement. The farmer, by using the baker's own bread as a reference point, exposes the baker's attempt at deception.

Adapted from various versions on the internet.

Ponder this:

This story goes beyond simply advocating for honesty. It emphasizes the importance of fair exchange and the consequences of inconsistency. By holding ourselves to the same standards we expect from others, we cultivate trust and build stronger relationships.

Learning from Failure

A young reporter, eager to learn the secrets of success, interviews a seasoned entrepreneur.

"Sir," he asked politely, "what has been the secret of your success?"

The older man leaned back on his leather swivel chair, behind his shining mahogany desk, and replied, "Two words, son, two words: *right decisions*."

The reporter wrote it down. Then he asked another question. "And how do you learn to make right decisions, sir?"

The successful business man leaned back further and replied, "One word, son, one word: *experience*."

The reporter wrote this down, too, and then asked, "Well, sir, how do you acquire experience?"

The older man leaned forward over his desk and whispered conspiratorially, "Two words, son, two words: *wrong decisions*!"

Adapted from various versions on the internet.

Ponder this:

The path to success is rarely a straight line. While we strive to make wise decisions, setbacks and mistakes are inevitable. The key lies not in avoiding mistakes altogether, but in embracing them as opportunities for learning and growth. By reflecting on our mistakes and actively seeking lessons within them, we gain valuable knowledge and develop the judgment required to make better choices in the future.

True Friends

Along a quiet country lane lies a field where two horses graze. At first glance, they might seem like any other horses. But a closer look reveals a remarkable story of friendship.

One of the horses is blind. His kind owner has chosen to provide a loving home for him rather than have him put down. This act of compassion is heartwarming in itself. However, a closer observation unveils something even more touching.

As you listen intently, a soft tinkling sound reaches your ears. Following the sound, you see a small bell attached to the bridle of the other, smaller horse. This bell acts as a guide for her blind companion, letting him know her location so he can follow her safely.

Watching these two friends interact is a truly moving experience. The smaller horse frequently checks on the blind horse, who in turn listens for the reassuring ring of the bell and slowly walks towards it, trusting his companion completely.

This scene serves as a beautiful metaphor for true friendship. Just as the owner cares for the blind horse, God watches over us, even when we face challenges. He guides us through life's difficulties, sometimes placing others in our paths to offer support.

At times, we may find ourselves like the blind horse, relying on the gentle guidance of a friend's "bell." Conversely, we may be the guiding horse, offering unwavering support and a listening ear. True friends, like the horses in this tale, are a constant presence – a source of strength even when unseen.

Adapted from various versions on the internet.

Ponder this:

True friendship goes beyond simply solving problems for one another. It's a deeper connection, a willingness to walk beside each other through life's journey, in good times and bad. True friends are the steady bell that guides us and the unwavering presence that assures us we are never truly alone.

Expert on Religion

A scholar, well-versed in scripture but yearning for deeper spiritual progress, sought an enlightened master residing in the Himalayas. After a long journey, he reached the master's cave, brimming with excitement.

He prostrated himself and launched into a detailed account of his studies, practices, and perceived roadblocks. The master listened patiently.

When the man paused for a moment to catch his breath, the Master calmly said, "Let us have a cup of tea." Confused, the scholar exclaimed, "Tea, Master? I've travelled for weeks on foot to reach you! I have spent years seeking enlightenment! Now, at your holy feet, I crave your wisdom, not tea!"

Unfazed, the master calmly laid out two cups for tea. He then began to pour tea from a kettle into each cup. As he filled the scholar's cup, the man observed that the Master continued pouring into his cup even as it overflowed, spilling onto the floor.

"Master, stop!" the scholar cried. "The cup is full! Can't you see the tea is spilling? There is no more room in the cup."

The master smiled and stopped pouring. "You are like this cup, my child. Just as the cup is so full that it can hold no more tea, you too are overflowing with your own ego, knowledge, stories, and explanations, leaving no room for anything else. My teachings cannot enter. Empty yourself – your preconceived notions, bookish knowledge, and interpretations – until you hold nothing. Only then can you receive what I offer."

Adapted from various versions on the internet.

Ponder this:

This story teaches us about staying humble and being open to new learning experiences. There are some folks who read a lot of spiritual books and think they know it all. But Jillellamudi Amma, a great sage of modern India, used to say, "*Experience teaches more than books ever could.*" This implies that experiencing things firsthand imparts insight that cannot be matched by reading books. Knowledge from books can be a little stale, but experience is ever new like a fresh adventure.

The Power of Focus

Arjuna, the third son of Queen Kunti, was an archer known for his passion and dedication. He practiced tirelessly, becoming the finest archer in his land. His teacher, Gurudev, favored him, which made his two older brothers jealous.

One day, the brothers openly accused Gurudev of being biased. To settle the matter, Gurudev set up a test to find the best archer. He placed a wooden bird on a distant tree, partly concealed by branches. The challenge was to shoot an arrow through the bird's eye.

Gurudev first invited the eldest son to shoot. Before he released his arrow, Gurudev asked, "O eldest son of Queen Kunti, what do you see?"

The eldest son replied, "I see you, the tree, the bird, and the people around us."

"Shoot," said Gurudev.

The eldest son took aim but missed.

Next, Gurudev called the second son to demonstrate his skill. Before he released his arrow, Gurudev asked, "O second son of Queen Kunti, what do you see?"

Anticipating a more targeted answer, he quickly replied, "I see the tree and the bird."

"Shoot," Gurudev instructed. He, too, missed.

Then it was Arjuna's turn. Gurudev asked, "O Arjuna, what do you see?"

"I see only the eye of the bird," Arjuna replied.

"Do you see the tree, the bird, or the people around you?" Gurudev asked.

"No," Arjuna responded. "I see only the bird's eye."

"Shoot," said Gurudev. Arjuna let his arrow fly, hitting the bird right in the eye.

"Well done," said Gurudev. He explained to the others that Arjuna's success was due to his intense focus, which gave him the advantage. It was his singular concentration that made him the best student.

~ Mahabharatha

Ponder this:

This classic tale from the Mahabharata illustrates the importance of singular focus in achieving mastery. Arjuna, a skilled archer, exemplifies this principle.

Arjuna's brothers, despite their technical skills, struggled to hit the target because their attention was divided. They saw the entire scene – the tree, the people, the bird. Arjuna, however, achieved a state of focused awareness. He saw only the target – the eye of the bird – and everything else faded away.

This laser focus allows him to hit the mark with precision, earning him the teacher's praise.

This story goes beyond mere focus on a physical object. It highlights how focusing our mental energy can have a transforming effect. When we train our attention on a desired outcome, blocking out distractions, we unlock a higher level of skill and effectiveness. Arjuna's accomplishment isn't just about archery; it's a metaphor for success in any endeavor. By harnessing the power of focused attention, we can achieve remarkable feats.

A Big Favour, please!

Dear Reader

Thank you for embarking on the inspiring journey of "*100+ Inspirational Short Stories About Success and Happiness.*" I hope you found the stories as impactful as I did. Did a story spark a new dream… or leave you feeling empowered?

Your thoughts on the book are invaluable, especially to others seeking to improve their lives. By sharing your insights in a review, you become a conduit for positive change.

Unfortunately, only a tiny fraction of readers leave reviews. As a self-published author, I don't have the promotional power of a big publishing company. Instead, I rely on valued readers like you to spread the word about the potential impact of the life lessons woven into these short stories.

Imagine *your words* igniting inspiration in someone else's life. By leaving a review, you're doing just that, and helping create a ripple effect of transformation that can touch countless other lives. Here's how you can make a difference:

1. Go to Amazon or www.Chosen4u.com/vra/
2. Select "100+ Inspirational Short Stories About Success and Happiness."
3. Scroll down to "Customer reviews," click "Write a customer review," and share your honest thoughts

Your review doesn't need to be lengthy; it just needs to reflect your truth.

Thank you for being part of this meaningful journey!

With heartfelt gratitude,
Verusha Robbins

P.S. If these short stories have left you eager to probe further into life's lessons, you'll love "*100+ Inspirational Poems and Prose about Life and Success.*" It's just as inspiring!

Our Gift To You

If you enjoyed this book, then you will find the following FREE publications just as enlightening:

- The 12 Best Inspirational Poems about Life and Success
- The Fastest Road to Success – The Secret Used by the World's Richest People to Double, Triple or Even 10X Their Income and Wealth
- My Journey to a Better Me – a short 12-module online course comprising a guide, printable journal and monthly planner for each module.

Go to www.Chosen4U.com/GiftsSS/ to access your free copies now.

Acknowledgements

This book's collection of stories and anecdotes has been gathered over two decades and sourced from various mediums, including emails, newsletters, online publications, and audio recordings. As with any anthology of quotations, tracing the origins of certain materials has presented challenges. While we have made every reasonable effort to attribute sources where possible, some have unfortunately remained obscure. We sincerely appreciate all those whose narratives have contributed to this work, even where precise citation has proven elusive.

Other resources by Verusha & Virend

Ready to go beyond the 100+ inspirational stories you just read?

The Inexplicable Laws of Success: Discover the Hidden Truths that Separate the 'Best' from the 'Rest' delves deeper, transforming those sparks of inspiration into a proven roadmap for achieving your dreams.

This groundbreaking book unveils the hidden truths that separate the consistently successful from the rest. It's not about magic formulas - it's about harnessing the power within you and aligning yourself with the universal principles that govern success.

Don't just be inspired, be empowered. Embark on a transformative journey with *The Inexplicable Laws of Success*. Your best self is waiting! Download for free from leading online bookstores.

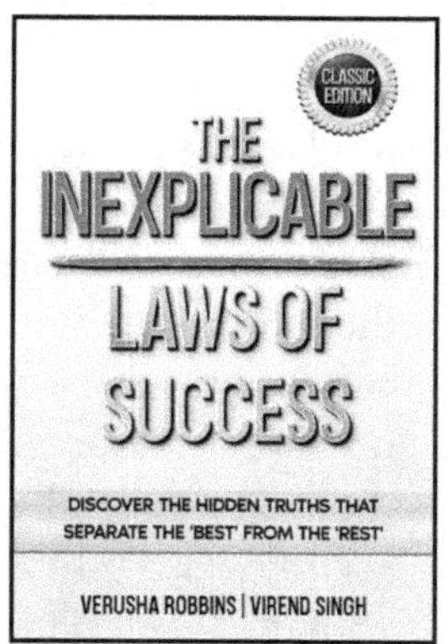
CLASSIC EDITION
THE
INEXPLICABLE
LAWS OF
SUCCESS
DISCOVER THE HIDDEN TRUTHS THAT
SEPARATE THE 'BEST' FROM THE 'REST'
VERUSHA ROBBINS | VIREND SINGH

PROFESSIONAL ENDORSEMENTS:

"This book gives ideas and insights into unlocking and releasing your full potential for happiness and success."

- Brian Tracy, International Best-Selling Author

100+ Inspirational Poems and Prose about Life and Success: Thought-provoking and Empowering Words to Uplift and Inspire You contains an impressive collection of insightful poetry that will touch your heart, give you hope and motivate you to be your best. The poems provide a powerful source of wisdom and inspiration and will make a great addition to any self-improvement or motivational book collection. It is a great resource for speakers, coaches, teachers, leaders and parents.

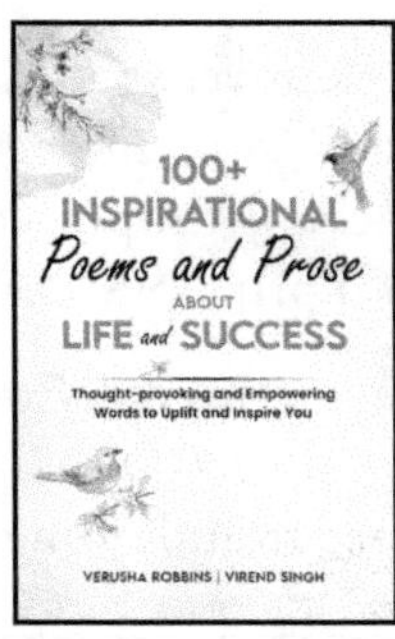

Inspirational Words and Positive Quotes to Live By: An Insightful Collection of Motivational Quotes is packed with wisdom and serve to remind you that life can be good, no matter what challenges you may be facing. These quotes will empower and encourage you to live your life to the fullest. They come from accomplished people, sages, philosophers and thinkers, all of whom started out as an ordinary citizen and have achieved greatness.

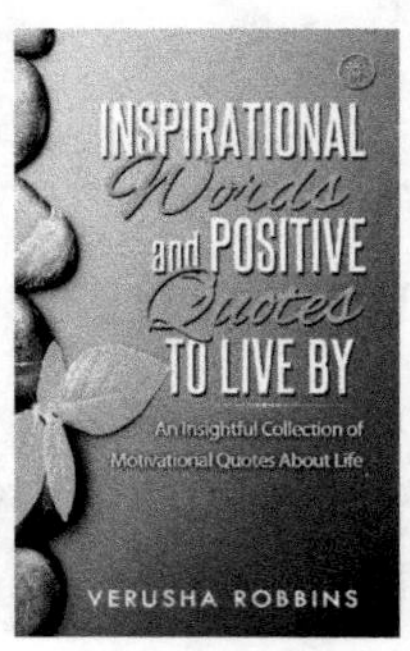

About The Authors

This book is the collaborative effort of Virend and Verusha, a father and daughter team.

Verusha Robbins is an accomplished writer and entrepreneur who thrives at both, captivating audiences with fictional narratives that entertain, as well as empowering others through personal transformation. Her expertise in Media & Writing and Editing & Publishing fuels her success in both realms. Her professional journey includes pivotal roles at esteemed publishing companies like Hay House (Australia). Looking ahead, Verusha remains committed to weaving captivating worlds through fiction while equipping readers with the knowledge they need to flourish in all aspects of life.

Virend Singh, a seasoned entrepreneur with an MBA, leverages his years of experience to empower others. His journey, marked by both triumphs and challenges, has instilled in him a deep understanding of the mindset and behaviors that drive high achievers. Drawing on these firsthand insights, Virend collaborates with his daughter, Verusha, in a unique father-daughter team. Together, they empower individuals to unlock their full potential, achieving success in both personal and professional realms.

For fans of fantasy...

If you are drawn to fantasy, in particular dark romance fantasy, then you will truly enjoy Verusha's latest novels:

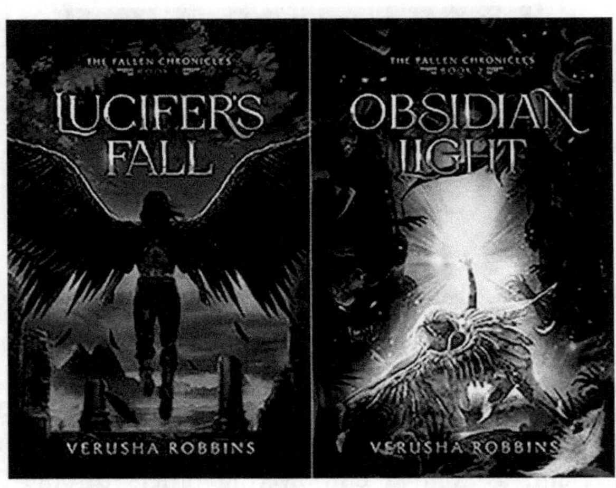

If you love the intricate world-building in Sarah J. Maas, Carissa Broadbent, and Anne Bishop's works, prepare to be mesmerized by these books.

Step into a spellbinding realm where angels and demons clash in an epic saga. Sandriel, a fallen angel with a mysterious past, is ensnared in a perilous dance with Lucifer, the most mesmerizing fallen angel of all. Her mission is clear: rescue the captive warrior angels in Hell and combat the Fallen, all while resisting the overwhelming allure of the Devil himself.

Themes to Captivate You:

- Enemies to Lovers
- Hell and Angels

- Captivity and Liberation
- Greek Mythology
- Emotional Healing and Scars
- Revenge and Redemption

Prepare for an exhilarating journey brimming with multifaceted characters, forbidden love, and jaw-dropping twists that will keep you reading late into the night.

Readers are enthralled by "Lucifer's Fall" and "Obsidian Light":

- "A masterpiece of storytelling. I couldn't put it down!"
- "The twists and turns are mind-blowing!"
- "I haven't been this captivated by a book in years!"
- "This book is 'unputdownable,' unique, and mysteriously beautiful."

Free Sample Available!

Download the first six chapters of "Lucifer's Fall" for free and discover why readers can't get enough. Visit www.chosen4u.com/LF6

Available now on all major platforms.

For more resources by Verusha and Virend go to

www.inkNivory.com/resources/

and

www.CoolSelfHelpTips.com

References

Books:

Braden, G (2006). *Secrets of the Lost Mode of Prayer: The Hidden Power of Beauty, Blessings, Wisdom, and Hurt.* San Diego: Hay House.

Chopra, D (1993). *Creating Affluence: Wealth Consciousness in the Field of All Possibilities.* New World Library Walk Your Talk With Praxis / Amber-Allen Publishing.

Halberstam, Y and Leventhal, J (1997). *Small Miracles: Extraordinary Coincidences from Everyday Life.* Adams Media Corporation. p18-19.

Hill, Napoleon (2014). *Think and Grow Rich.* CreateSpace Independent Publishing Platform. p 17

Kersey, C (1998). *Unstoppable: 45 Powerful Stories of Perseverance and Triumph from People Just Like You.* Sourcebooks, Inc.

Kiyosaki, Robert T (2000). *Rich Dad's Cashflow Quadrant: Rich Dad's Guide to Financial Freedom.* Business Plus; Later Printing edition

Major, John S, Queen, Sarah, Meyer, Andrew & Roth, D. Harold (2010). *The Huainanzi: A Guide to the Theory and Practice of Government in Early Han China (Translations from the Asian Classics).* Columbia University Press

Mandino, Og (1990). *A Better Way to Live: Og Mandino's Own Personal Story of Success Featuring 17 Rules to Live By.* Bantam, pg 11-17

Murphy, J (2001). *The Power of Your Subconscious Mind.* Bantam.

Pearsall, P (1999). *The Heart's Code: Tapping the Wisdom and Power of Our Heart Energy.* Broadway Books

Pritchett, Price (PhD) 2012. *you²: A High Velocity Formula for Multiplying Your Personal Effectiveness in Quantum Leaps.* Pritchett LP; Rep edition (February 1, 2012)

Vyasa, Krishna-Dwaipayana (2013). *The Complete Mahabharata (Volume 3 of 4, Books 8 to 12).* Digireads.com

Waitley, Dennis (1992). *Timing Is Everything.* Thomas Nelson Inc

Ziglar, Zig (1975). *See You at the Top.* Pelican Books, p 199

Internet:

Alessandra, Tony Dr. *A Leader Always Fails Upwards!* Available: http://www.alessandra.com/timelytips/28.asp. Last accessed 26th August 2015.

Asthana, Kishore. *Advice for Couples – Be like the Cashew Nut and not like the Walnut.* Available: https://sanitybalance.in/?s=Advice+for+couples. Last accessed 4th April 2024.

Baltazar-Schwartz, Francie. *A Positive Attitude Makes Everything Different.* Available: http://www.motivateus.com/stories/attitu.htm. Last accessed 25th August 2015.

Baba, Sai. (2005). *Suitable Hiding Place.* Available: http://groups.yahoo. com/group/saibabanews/message/7356. Last accessed 3rd November 2011.

Clarita (2011). *Inspiring Short Stories.* Available: http://www.mdjunction.com/forums/positive-thinking-discussions/general-support/2792572-inspiring-short-stories. Last accessed 12th September 2015

Coelho, Paulo. (2003). *The Meaning of Peace.* Available: https://www.melanieslibrary.com/the-real-meaning-of-peace/. Last accessed 4th April 2024.

Coelho, Paulo. (2009). *The story of the pencil.* Available: http://paulocoelhoblog.com/2009/12/19/the-story-of-the-pencil/. Last accessed 5th September 2015.

Doolan, Marion (1970). *"Lady, Are You Rich?".* Available: https://www.scribd.com/document/671663881/Lady-are-you-rich. Last accessed 4th April 2024.

Elan (2014). *Two Seeds (Wisdom).* Available: https://mythologystories.wordpress.com/2014/01/14/2seeds/. Last accessed 4th April 2024.

Elliot, Elisabeth (1995*). The Missing Contact Lens.* Available: https://www.snopes.com/fact-check/the-ant-and-the-contact-lens/. Last accessed 4th April 2024

Fares, Aymen (2011). *Twins – A Parable.* Available: http://www.spiritual.com.au/2011/07/twins-a-parable/. Last accessed 4th April 2024

Freedman, Rav Binny. *A weekly Byte … from Isralight.* Available: http://www.isralight.org/assets/Text/RBF_kitisah06.html. Last accessed 4th April 2024

Harricharan, J. *The Power of Giving.* Available: http://www.courses-free.com/spiritual-e-book.html

Hoff, Naphtali (2017). *To Be Successful, Burn Your Boats.* Available: https://www.success.com/to-be-successful-burn-your-boats/?mpweb=574-7381273-658253089. Last accessed 4th April 2024.

How Would You Like To Be Remembered? Available: https://www.history.com/news/did-a-premature-obituary-inspire-the-nobel-prize. Last accessed 12th April 2024.

Jeftovic, Mark (2013). *The Tragedy Contrarianism.* Available: http://rebootingcapitalism.com/2013/03/05/the-tragedy-of-contrarianism/. Last accessed 12th September 2015.

Josephson, Michael (2012). Commentary 778.3: The Parable of Brother Leo. Available: http://whatwillmatter.com/2012/06/commentary-778-3-brother-leo-servant-leadership/. Last accessed 31st August 2015.

Lee, Bruce (2007). *Wisdom of Yoda, Bruce Lee.* Available: https://st4rbux.wordpress.com/2007/08/08/wisdom-of-yoda-bruce-lee/. Last accessed 31st August 2015.

Lundstrom, M. (1996). *A Wink from the Cosmos.* Available: http://www. flowpower.com/synchro.htm. Last accessed 4th Jan 2011.

Mali, Taylor. (2011). *What Teachers Makes.* Available: http://www.taylormali.com/?s=what+do+you+make&submit=Search Last accessed 2nd October 2015

Randolph, Keith. (2002). *Sports Visualizations.* Available: https://www.llewellyn.com/encyclopedia/article/244. Last accessed 2nd October 2015.

Rao, Prof. Srikumar. *Lessons From a Snow Globe.* Available: https://theraoinstitute.com/lessons-from-a-snow-globe-and-other-insights/. Last accessed 2nd April 2024.

Saraswati, Swami Chidanand. (2004). *Guru Purnima Blessings from Pujya Swamiji.* Available: http://www.ihrf.com/messages/guru-purnima2004.html. Last accessed: 12th September 2015

Shah, Idries. (1969). Tales of the Dervishes: Teaching-stories of the Sufi Masters over the past thousand years. Available: http://www.ratical.org/ratville/JFK/TalesOfTheDervishes.pdf. Last accessed: 2nd October 2015

Stockton, Frank (1882). *The Lady or the Tiger.* Available: https://leavesandpages.com/2012/09/10/review-the-lady-or-the-tiger-and-other-stories-by-frank-stockton/. Last accessed 5th April 2024

Sylvia, C. (2008). *I was given a young man's heart - and started craving beer and Kentucky Fried Chicken. My daughter said I even walked like a man.* Available: http://www.dailymail.co.uk/health/article-558256/. Last accessed 4th July 2000

The Emperor And The Seed. (2011). Available: http://islam.ru/en/content/story/emperor-and-seed. Last accessed 12th September 2015

The Hundredth Monkey Phenomenon. (2009). Available: http://www.storiesofwisdom.com/the-hundredth-monkey-phenomenon/. Last accessed 4th May 2011.

The Tunnel. (2014). Available: https://dsjenessa.blogspot.com/2014/03/the-tunnel.html. Last accessed 4th April 2024.

The Weight of the Glass. (2014). Available: https://www.laoistoday.ie/2022/11/12/fr-paddy-byrne-the-weight-of-the-glass/. Last accessed 4th April 2024.

Tugend, Alina. (2010). *Too Many Choices: A Problem That Can Paralyze.* Available: http://www.nytimes.com/2010/02/27/your-money/27shortcuts.html?_r=1 Last accessed 12th September 2015.

Unknown. *Thinking "Out of the Box".* Available: https://authorbeckyjohnen.wordpress.com/2020/01/12/thinking-outside-the-box/. Last accessed 5th April 2024

Unknown. (2010). *Lessons Learnt in (Re)Morse Code.* Available: https://archive.sssmediacentre.org/journals/Vol_01/07Dec01/10_KINDLE_YOUR_SPIRIT/02_LESSONS/Lessons.htm. Last accessed 4th April 2024.

Widemark, S. (2009). *Lessons From The Geese.* Available: http://suewidemark.com/lessonsgeese.htm. Last accessed 20th Dec 2011.

Audio

Tracy, Brian (1993). *Maximum Achievement.* Simon & Schuster Audio

www.ingramcontent.com/pod-product-compliance
Lightning Source LLC
LaVergne TN
LVHW051627080426
835511LV00016B/2220

* 9 7 8 1 9 2 2 1 1 3 4 0 5 *